NORTON, Paul

The spirit of love

PIATKUS

First published in Great Britain in 2008 by Piatkus Books

Copyright © Paul Norton and Tracy Hall

A CIP catalogue record for this book
is available from the British Library

ISBN 978-0-7499-2848-3

Papers used by Piatkus are natural, recyclable products made
from wood grown in sustainable forests and certified in accordance
with the rules of the Forest Stewardship Council

Typeset in Adobe Garamond by
Action Publishing Technology Ltd, Gloucester

Printed and bound in Great Britain by
Mackays Ltd, Chatham, Kent

Edited by Kelly Davis
Text Design by Briony Hartley

CONTENTS

For Peter, Nigel and Tony, who taught
us many lessons, but most importantly
the truth about life and death.

Blessed are they that mourn:
for they shall be comforted.
Matthew 5:4

ACKNOWLEDGEMENTS

We would like to say a huge thank you to the many people who have helped and supported us along the way:

Special thanks go to those who inspired us to seek out the truth: Doris Collins, who has featured significantly in our story from start to finish, and Gordon Higginson, an inspiration to us all. Their tireless work on behalf of the spirit world, enthusiasm, knowledge and guidance, has been a blessing to us.

To those who played a part in helping us to develop our gifts – Sandy, Edie, Phillip, Chris and Matt – we thank you all for your patience and understanding.

We would also like to thank those who have played a significant role in helping us with *The Spirit of Love*:

To Roy Wooding, who took our first ever publicity photographs in 2002 and who is responsible for the front cover photograph of this book. Thanks, Roy – you did a brilliant job!

To Robert Kilroy Silk, for allowing us to use his article about Richard and Margaret. Thanks, Kilroy – we really appreciate your objective views and speedy response.

To Jeffrey Simmons, our wonderful literary agent, who believed in us and who has helped to make a wish come true.

Acknowledgements

Jeffrey – we couldn't have done it without you. You are the crucial piece of the jigsaw which made everything fit into place. We are proud to have you represent us, and prouder still to consider you our friend.

To Joan Deitch – who helped us in the initial stages, made us grammatically correct, and came up with so many helpful suggestions to spur us on.

To Helen Stanton – whose emails have popped onto our computer screens on a regular basis and whose tireless commitment and faith in our project has been the light at the end of the tunnel, when we were beginning to feel weary.

To Gill Bailey and Judy Piatkus for giving us a chance. We really appreciate it.

Thank you all.

And finally, for being our best friend ever through good times and bad, Little Bo, who died 25 April 2006. We miss your grumpy ways, but would give anything to have you back.

CHAPTER 1
Tracy: A friend in need

I awoke with a start. My heart was racing, my mouth was dry and I felt uneasy. I looked around the unfamiliar room, taking in the strange surroundings.

Then it all came flooding back to me – my dad had died two days before and it really hurt. Suddenly the silence was broken by the quiet voice of my friend and colleague Paul Norton.

'Feeling better, Tracy?' he asked, as I looked up, trying to hide my embarrassment. I had fallen asleep on Paul's sofa when we should have been discussing venues for our tour. We had been working together as mediums for just over a year, ever since fate had joined forces with destiny and brought us together.

I sat up, ran my fingers through my hair, and tried to shake off the feelings of exhaustion and despair that had over-whelmed me all weekend.

Paul lit a cigarette and walked over to the French doors. 'Don't worry, we'll talk about work tomorrow,' he said. 'The sleep will have done you good.'

I stood up unsteadily, ready to make my excuses and go home.

'Don't go,' Paul urged. 'We need to talk.'

I didn't feel like talking or socialising. I wanted to be on my own, to come to terms with Dad's passing. However, Paul was such a good friend I didn't want to hurt his feelings, so I waited patiently for him to continue.

'There's something I need to tell you,' he said. 'Whilst you were sleeping, a spirit man was standing next to you.'

'Who was it?' I asked quickly.

'I'm not sure at the moment,' Paul replied, inhaling deeply on his cigarette. 'All I can tell you is that I saw a man with a beard, but he told me he didn't have it when he died.'

I immediately recalled that my dad had had a beard a couple of years before but not at the end of his life. Paul had never met my father and I had rarely discussed my family with him during the year we had been friends, so I was very impressed with the information he was able to tell me during the next hour.

'I think this is your dad, Tracy,' Paul announced. 'He mentions Frank, Billy, Joe and Roy.'

'They're my uncles, Dad's brothers.' I confirmed.

'He's also talking about Marjorie and Charlie.'

'Yes,' I replied, 'that's his mum and dad.'

I was shocked. My dad had only died two days ago and yet here was Paul, giving me some quite startling evidence that he was here in the room with a message for me. I had tears in my eyes as I listened intently.

'He gives me the name Tomkins,' said Paul. I told him that this was the name of a delivery firm my dad had worked for.

Paul described my father's personality, as well as the clothes he wore and his hairstyle. He mentioned a photograph of my dad wearing a cowboy hat; I knew the one he meant. Paul told me that Dad enjoyed gardening, and had worked as a taxi driver – this was all correct. I could scarcely believe it; this was pretty amazing stuff!

Paul continued: 'He's talking about Christine, the surname Moss, and also Ronnie.'

Mum and dad had divorced some years before; Christine Moss was dad's girlfriend, and Ronnie her ex-husband.

'He's telling me about a family connection with Grimsby and also Ollerton,' Paul said.

'Yes, my dad was born in Grimsby, and Ollerton was where his parents moved to,' I replied.

Everything I was being told was so pertinent – and to receive such a message so soon after Dad's death was quite astonishing. However it wasn't over yet. Paul lit another cigarette, and then went on to say, 'He's telling me that he's with someone called Wilf.' Wilf was my other grandad, my mum's father.

Paul then described Dad's flat and made reference to some false teeth in a kitchen cupboard. This was the only thing I was unsure of: as far as I was aware, there weren't any false teeth at Dad's flat. I knew, however, that there was a set at the nursing home where Dad had been when he died. Eventually, the message ended with Dad telling Paul to say that I was to keep up the good work, and that he had been watching over me on Friday night. I went home feeling elated.

The weeks leading up to this night had been very difficult for me. Paul had helped me through it all. I had only found out in September that Dad was ill and here I was now, not only mourning his death, but receiving a comforting

3

message from him. I couldn't thank Paul enough for everything he had done.

Facing the truth

I had found out about Dad's illness when I had felt compelled to go and visit him one Sunday evening in September. I hadn't been visiting him as often as usual because I had just moved, and was busy settling into my new home. On this particular day, something kept niggling away in the back of my mind, and so when I had finished all my jobs at home, I dropped everything and drove the 20 miles to visit him.

Dad was really pleased to see me, but I was shocked when I saw him. He looked weak and his skin was sallow. I also noticed that his clothes were loose. He was sitting in the dark alone, watching *Songs of Praise*, one of his favourite programmes. I felt so ashamed and upset that I hadn't been to see him before.

'Dad, you don't look very well,' I said. He just shrugged his shoulders and said he was fine.

'You don't look fine,' I insisted.

'Well I am,' he muttered. By this time, I was frustrated and urged him to tell me the truth.

'What's wrong with you?' I demanded. Eventually Dad told me that he had just been diagnosed with cancer of the bladder. He held me when I cried and told me not to worry because they could cure cancer nowadays. But I knew deep down that he was dying and there was nothing I could do. I vowed to myself that from now on I would try my best to help him, even though I had a few problems of my own at that time.

I had just left my husband of 16 years and embarked upon a new life, with my two children, Gemma and Luke, then aged 13 and 8. It was a real juggling act being a single parent, trying to hold down a new job in an estate agent's office during the day, and working with Paul as a medium at night – but our work was going so well, and for the first time in ages I really felt a sense of purpose in my life. Dad's illness couldn't have come at a worse time, but I was especially close to him, and knew I would find the strength from somewhere to see that he was happy during the last months or weeks of his life.

After hearing Dad's devastating news, I sat with him a while, and was amazed by his positive attitude and his determination to overcome the cancer. I didn't want to leave him, but knew I had to get back home for the kids, and so we reluctantly said our goodbyes. When I got back I immediately phoned Paul. He tried to reassure me, but I realised from the sound of his voice that he wasn't too optimistic either. I spent the next few days making enquiries to find out what would happen and what support was available. I arranged for a social worker to visit, but Dad was reluctant to accept any help. I respected his decision, and so we muddled through those last few weeks together.

Luckily, my dad was living in sheltered accommodation at the time and the warden there was really helpful. She kept a close eye on him whenever I wasn't around. I wanted to do my best for everyone, but felt pulled in a million directions and became totally worn out.

Dad certainly gave me a few hair-raising moments during those last weeks. One night he was suffering from palpitations in his chest, and in a great deal of pain he rang me, asking me to take him to hospital. I rushed over to Retford to pick him up and take him to the Outpatients Department at Worksop. When we arrived he was asked to strip off while the doctor examined him. After that he was placed in a cubicle with a heart monitor attached. He suddenly became desperate to urinate (as he had cancer of the bladder, this was quite a problem for him) so I went to get a nurse to help him.

Imagine my horror when I returned, and saw Dad running down the corridor naked, and jumping into the next bed, where he quickly made himself comfortable. Unfortunately he had wet the other one, whilst I was seeking help. I wanted to tell him off but couldn't – the whole episode was so comical, and the nurses didn't see it as a problem; in fact, they were brilliant. Dad was admitted to hospital that night, which meant that, for the next week, I was travelling regularly to Worksop to see him.

Saying goodbye

In October he was taken into the local hospice. This was a beautiful place of peace and tranquillity. He loved it there; but his condition had deteriorated rapidly. He began to contemplate the thought of dying and often spoke to me about how he wanted his affairs to be sorted out after he had gone. He handed me his bank cards and asked that everything be divided equally between my brother, my sister and me. He was slightly afraid of what the afterlife might bring, and I'm certain he was scared of dying in his sleep, as he insisted on the television in his room never being switched off.

Two weeks later, he was moved to a nursing home. At this

point he was in a great deal of pain and for most of the time he was sleepy because of all the medication he was being given. He decided at this time that he would like a DVD player. I went and bought him one, along with a selection of DVDs, but he never got to watch them because he was too ill.

His best times were in the mornings. I would call round to the nursing home straight after dropping the kids off at school and he would happily chat away whilst having his breakfast. The last time he was alert and able to chat like this was about three days before he died. That morning, my mum had accompanied me to the nursing home, and Dad asked for yoghurt for his breakfast.

He let me feed him, as by this time he was too weak to feed himself. After a bit of a chat he went to sleep. That was the last time I saw him awake. That same night we were all called to the nursing home. The staff were concerned as Dad's breathing had altered, and they expected him to pass over at any time. For the next three days, we all kept a vigil at his bedside, and watched him slowly fade away before our eyes. We passed the hours chatting and reminiscing about old times. The nurses were brilliant, and we enjoyed sharing ghost stories in the middle of the night – the staff were convinced that the place was haunted.

On the Friday of that week I was supposed to be working in Selby with Paul. I'd rung him in the morning and told him that I might not be able to make it. He had told me not to worry and that he would explain to the audience what was happening. At two o'clock that afternoon, after keeping a bedside vigil for three days and nights I was extremely tired and I decided that I would return home for a couple of hours' sleep. There had been no change in Dad's condition over the last 24 hours and so I had no reason to suspect that anything untoward would happen whilst I was gone. At three o'clock precisely, my brother Adrian telephoned to tell me that Dad had just died.

I immediately drove back to Retford to see Dad at rest. He looked peaceful and there was a gentle smile on his lips. I wished him goodbye and left.

As I drove home I was overwhelmed by immense feelings of loneliness. I had been close to my dad and knew I would miss him terribly. Checking the time, I realised that I could still make it to Selby with Paul. I rang him and explained that Dad had died and I didn't want to be alone. We agreed that I would go along and sit in the audience and Paul would do the evening on his own.

At 7.30 p.m. Paul walked out onto the stage to rapturous applause. He was well known in the town and the audience was looking forward to seeing him. He started by explaining to everyone about my dad, and saying that I probably wouldn't be joining him on stage that night. However, when he announced the interval, I knew that I wanted to work in the second half. It was almost as if I could hear my dad telling me not to be sad and to get out there and show them what I could do. Dad had never seen me work as a medium, although he knew about what I did and often asked about it. I walked into the dressing room and told Paul that I wanted to give it a go.

He was reluctant at first, as he wasn't sure if, under the circumstances, I was strong enough to face an audience, but we agreed I would try, and if there were any problems, he would take over for me. Paul went out first in the second half to explain what was happening, and he was quite emotional as he told the audience that I had specifically asked if I could work as planned that night. As I walked out onto the stage, everyone stood up and clapped. People whistled and cheered as I stood there waiting for them to settle.

I explained that I hadn't slept for three days and nights, but that I would do my best for them. Everything went well, and I am certain that my dad was there with me, helping me every step of the way.

The day after Paul's message from my dad I went with my mum and my brother Adrian to empty Dad's flat. At the precise moment that I opened the kitchen cupboard and found a spare set of false teeth, my mobile phone rang. It was Paul, ringing to remind me about the teeth!

The message I received through Paul really helped me come to terms with Dad's death, and get myself back on track again. This was mediumship at its best, and once again, I was so grateful to everyone in the spirit world for helping me to meet and work with Paul. I am sure they played a very big part in the coincidences, twists and turns in our lives that eventually brought us together.

Working with Paul

Paul's expertise as a medium often amazed me. His message from my dad was further confirmation that he was one of the best mediums in the country and I was determined that I wouldn't let him down. However, when he had first asked me to work with him a year earlier, in October 2001, it had taken all his powers of persuasion to get me to agree.

The reason I had been so reluctant in the beginning was that I lacked confidence. When I met Paul, I was doing well as a medium in the Spiritualist churches, but his suggestion that I progress to working in theatres alongside him frightened the life out of me. When I asked him why he wanted me to work with him, Paul replied that he knew it was the right thing to do. In the end I agreed to do three evenings with him, to see how it went.

As the date of our first meeting approached, I became extremely nervous. Paul had worked with other mediums in the past – some of them very famous, such as Doris Collins, Gordon Higginson and Colin Fry. I didn't feel I could match up to any of these and must have driven Paul mad, changing my mind on a regular basis about whether I could go through with it all. Soon, however, it was too late; the venues were booked, and the night of our first demonstration arrived.

We were working in Chesterfield, and there were about 100 people present. Paul felt it would be better if I went first, as I was the more nervous. He introduced me to the audience and I stood up to speak, pacing nervously up and down as I explained what would happen when the spirit people started to come through.

I remember hesitantly shouting out that I needed to speak to someone whose father had been in the police force. A lady raised her hand, and I delivered a message from the man, who had passed suddenly with a heart attack. For my second message I pointed towards a gentleman sitting on my left-hand side. I told him there was a young boy with me who was his son. This young boy had passed away with leukaemia and had needed an oxygen mask just before he passed over. I described the hospital room he had lain in, and how he had marks on his arms from the drips. I gave the date and time he had passed away, and mentioned the names of those people who had been with him when he went.

The gentleman in the audience was overcome, and began to cry. He left the hall and went to buy a whiskey from the bar to help calm himself down. At the end of the evening, he came to thank me and told me that his son had died only two weeks before.

Paul also gave some first-rate messages that night, amazing the audience with names and addresses of the spirit people who had come to talk. On the way home, he told me that he thought I was an excellent medium, and that he knew he had made the right choice in asking me to work with him. I went to bed that night feeling pleased that I hadn't backed out.

Jean and Annie

Our next meeting was a couple of weeks later at Kirkby in Ashfield in Nottinghamshire. We arrived at the venue about an hour before we were due to start, and there was a crowd of more than 100 eager people waiting to get into the building. I was petrified. I didn't work as well that night as I had at Chesterfield, but this was more down to nerves than anything else. Paul, however, was magnificent and we received many e-mails and letters afterwards enquiring when we would be returning to Mansfield.

Our final demonstration of the year was in Maltby, South Yorkshire. Again, over 100 people were packed into a tiny hall. From the minute we started speaking, there was a great 'buzz' about our work but the audience members that night were really the stars of the show.

I remember giving a message to a young woman whose aunty had passed away with breast cancer and who happily chatted to her niece about the fact that she had carried on smoking right until the end of her life. She then said that her niece had been badly hurt by a former boyfriend, and took great pleasure in informing everyone that she had never really liked this chap, and that she was much better off without him. She went on to talk about her niece's new boyfriend, whom she named, and who she stated was 'the best she'd ever had'. At this point, the young woman's friend shouted out for all to hear: 'She hasn't had him yet!' After which everyone burst out laughing and it took a great deal of effort on my part to calm them down. I remember looking towards Paul at the back of the hall: he was smirking and trying not to catch my eye.

It is amazing how the spirit communicators come through with their different personalities and can lift everyone's mood with a simple, but pithy comment.

After the event in Maltby, we were approached by a gentleman who told us that his sister desperately needed a private sitting. I discovered that her name was Jean, and that she lived in Sheffield. I agreed to meet her the following Sunday as I was booked to take a church service at Whitham Road Spiritualist Church. Paul was unable to join me as he was taking a church service in Peterborough that day.

Jean sat patiently through my service, then I ushered her into the mediums' room at the back of the church so we could spend some private time together.

The sitting didn't seem to start too well.

I described Jean's parents with pertinent details of their lives. She agreed I was correct, but it was apparent that this was not who she had wanted to hear from. They talked of there being five grandchildren. Jean looked shocked when I said this, and seemed upset.

I gave her the name Annie, and said that there was a young woman in the spirit world who wished to make contact. Jean acknowledged this. I tried to find out in my mind who this young woman was, but made a bit of a bad job of it. I knew it was someone very close indeed, as I wanted to place her directly by Jean's side, like a close friend or sister, but I didn't actually get the fact that Annie was her daughter until Jean told me.

However, the other information that came out was quite amazing, and sent shivers down my spine as I was saying it.

I told Jean that Annie had died in a tragic accident, and it transpired that she had died in a fire. I told Jean that she had photographs of her daughter all over the house – even in the bathroom. All of this was correct.

I then told her that Annie had been feeling depressed about her appearance, and that she had confided this to her mother, who had taken her to the doctor. I told Jean that as a child Annie had had a selection of 'My Little Pony' toys, which were still kept in a box.

I mentioned a connection with Wickersley, near Rotherham, and the surname of Rogers. (Jean's family were from Wickersley and her maiden name was Rogers.)

Afterwards, Jean thanked me for what had come through, and told me that her daughter had actually been called

Anneka, but that everyone called her Annie, so this was the best proof she could have wished for. She said she could have listened to me all afternoon. We agreed to keep in touch, and Jean said the next time I was working in Sheffield, I could go to her house for tea, which I did.

Jean had a lovely house on the outskirts of Sheffield with wonderful views. She showed me the photographs of her daughter, in particular in the bathroom, where one whole wall was dedicated to photos of Annie. She made me giggle when she brought out a little book, where she had kept a record of all the readings she had had from different mediums. She had given each one a score, and made comments about what had been said. Luckily, my message had been one of the better ones!

After that, I didn't hear from Jean for a while. We seemed to lose touch, until one night in July 2003, when Paul and I were due to take a meeting in Rotherham. I couldn't seem to get Jean out of my mind, and during the day I mentioned to Paul that I hoped she might turn up tonight to see us, as it would be lovely to chat to her again, and maybe give her a message from her daughter. It was almost as if I could feel Anneka close to me, wanting to make contact.

Before the start of the meeting, I noticed Jean's brother walking in through the door. I immediately jumped up and ran over to him, giving him a big hug. I asked him if Jean was with him. He took me to one side and told me that he had come to let me know that Jean was dead. She had contracted lung cancer – and since Anneka had gone she hadn't had the will to live, 80 she had died of a broken heart. He told me that she would have wanted me to know that she had gone, as she had thought a great deal about me, and had held me in very high esteem for the kindness I had shown her.

Jean's brother thanked me for everything I had done for his sister. Taking my hand, he shook it vigorously and sadly. I haven't seen him since.

From strength to strength

After we had done those first three meetings together at the end of 2001, my confidence had grown and Paul persuaded me to try a few more.

We spent the Christmas break of 2001 searching for venues around the country, and soon had quite a few events booked in for the coming year. One of the first demonstrations we did in February was at a theatre in Barnsley. We knew that the tickets were sold out prior to the event and were in high spirits as we travelled over to the venue. Another 70 disappointed people turned up to see us that night, all of whom we had to turn away as they hadn't bought tickets in advance. Whilst I was working during the first half, Paul was outside trying to calm down the crowd, who were furious that no seats were available for them to see these 'amazing mediums' they had heard so much about.

Later that year, we were at a venue in Lincolnshire, and Paul was busy setting up the table whilst I was downstairs in a little side room 'tuning in' to the spirit world. All of a sudden, I heard heavy footsteps running across the length of the great hall upstairs. Paul shouted at me several times, to hurry up and come and help him. There was a huge crowd outside, frantically banging on the doors to be let in. That night we had to turn another 30 people away, as the hall wasn't big enough to accommodate them all.

The next few months followed the same pattern. Wherever we went, we were inundated with people queuing to see us work. Eventually I got used to it, but I really did suffer from nerves and often Paul had to quite literally push me out onto the stage. Luckily, though, the spirit world never let me down, and people from all around the country wrote to say thank you for the messages they had received through my mediumship.

At the same time, another challenge was thrown at me. Paul and I were invited to appear on a local radio station, called Hallam FM. We were booked in to appear on the extremely popular *Diana Luke Show* and give messages live on air. Boy, did the thought of that give me some sleepless nights! Eventually, however, the big day came around and we arrived at the Hallam FM studios. Paul was very relaxed, as he had broadcast from a number of radio stations in the past, as well as appearing on television with such famous people as David Frost, Siân Phillips; Toyah Willcox and Robert Kilroy Silk. Diana Luke was brilliant: she immediately put us at ease, and we sailed through the first part of the show, talking about ourselves as mediums and then about our work together. Eventually it was time to take some calls from listeners, and imagine my shock when the first young man who called in said he would prefer to talk to me!

My mouth went dry, and then all of a sudden I launched into a message from his grandmother, telling him that he was gay and that he had just 'come out' to his family. He burst into tears at the other end of the phone, and I asked if it was all right to continue with such a personal message. He urged me to go on. I told him that he had informed five people that week about his sexuality, but that there was still one other to tell – this was his sister and I gave her name. I described his bedroom to him and told him that his grandmother had been with him during the early hours of the morning when he had been crying because he felt so alone. I proved this to him, by telling him he had stood up and opened a window and, as he did so, he thought he had seen his grandmother out of the corner of his eye. He confirmed this. I told him how his grandmother had passed to the spirit world and gave her date of passing. I also mentioned the dates of close family birthdays, and advised him that he was looking for a new job. He stated that everything I had said was true.

After this, the phone lines became jammed with people telephoning in to speak to us both, so much so that Diana asked us to join her again to do another live phone-in a couple of weeks later.

We have since appeared on a number of radio shows and featured in many newspaper articles. We have also been lucky enough to work together on Sky Television, and are often approached by TV companies who want to feature us in their programmes about psychics and mediums.

Of course, it was hard for me when Dad became ill in 2002 and later passed away. I openly admit that it was difficult for me to do my work as a medium whilst I was still grieving, but with Paul's friendship and support I found a way to get through it.

During the six years we have known each other, it has become apparent that our initial meeting may not have been down to chance after all, but more a question of fate. Some people may find it difficult to believe in fate and destiny, but our experiences have shown us that anything and everything is possible, provided that we as individuals embrace what life presents us with. Neither of us was particularly looking for the other and yet, as you will see, over a 20-year period our paths had crossed on more than one occasion. We now believe that fate shaped our early lives, and when the time was right destiny brought us together.

When Paul and I first met in August 2001, we soon discovered that we had many things in common, particularly the fact that we had both experienced a number of sad and unusual deaths within our families. We seemed to form an immediate bond, almost as if we had always known each other.

At that time my father was still alive, but my brother Nigel had recently taken his own life and I was still coming to terms with this tragic event. Paul confided that his dad had also taken his own life. He agreed with me that you never really understand why the ones you love choose to take this route, and it makes it all the more difficult for the people left behind to get over it.

Of course what *does* help is if you find a good medium who can deliver a message to you from your loved one, bringing you comfort and faith that you will be reunited with them in the future. This has always spurred me on with my own work as a medium, and I believe that through my own losses I have gained a great deal of empathy with others who are grieving.

Paul's message from my dad really helped me to overcome one of the saddest losses I have ever had to deal with. Unfortunately for Paul, when his dad died, he had to do a great deal more searching and questioning to find peace of mind.

I was lucky because, through Paul, my friend, my colleague and teacher, I was in the right place at the right time.

CHAPTER 2
Paul: A woman of spirit

I had never experienced anyone dying until I was 18 and then everything seemed to happen at once.

One night, I was just drifting off to sleep, when there was a commotion downstairs. Tony, my older brother, came running in and I heard Mum asking him what was wrong. He replied that Paul, a family friend, had been killed. For a few moments the house was silent. I made my way downstairs to the lounge where Mum and Dad were sitting. They looked dumbfounded.

Paul was like one of the family, so this news came as a terrible shock. We later discovered that he and some friends had been on their way to Skegness on their motorbikes. In Gainsborough, Paul had lost control of his bike on a notorious bend, and he and his passenger, Mick, had fallen off. Unfortunately, a car had been coming in the opposite direction and both Paul and Mick had slid underneath it. Paul was killed instantly; Mick sustained leg injuries and had to spend quite some time in hospital.

A strange thing happened afterwards. Whilst Mick was recovering, he told some visitors that Paul had been in to see him on the evening of the accident. At the time, the doctors thought it best not to tell Mick that Paul had been killed, so he had no idea that Paul had passed away and yet was perfectly sure he had seen him.

Some people obviously thought that Mick had imagined it, but I was intrigued. Until then, the only experience I had had of death was what I had witnessed on television or read about in newspapers. I'd never lost anyone close to me before and so had no real concept of grief. After Paul died, I remember finding it difficult to accept that one minute a person could be alive and the next 'dead'.

I'd never seen a dead body either. I was encouraged to go and see Paul, to help me come to terms with his death. At the Chapel of Rest, everyone commented on how different he looked. At first glance, you'd have thought he was merely sleeping, yet quite clearly there was something missing; that vibrant personality we had all known and loved wasn't there any more, even though the physical body was.

Hundreds turned up at the crematorium to pay their respects to this popular young man whose life had ended so tragically. The service only seemed to last a few minutes, after which the curtains at the altar began to close. This would be the last time any of us would be close to Paul's physical body. Everyone seemed totally overwhelmed with grief. No one was able to comprehend the tragic loss of such a young life.

We were all invited back to Paul's house after the service; there were so many people that some just stood in the driveway. Each time Paul's mother approached us, we smiled uneasily and bowed our heads as it became increasingly difficult to know what to say to her at such a sad time. After all, we were still alive, but her son was dead.

I visited Paul's mother as much as possible after the funeral, because I instinctively knew that this would be the time when she needed company. I often wonder if this was the foundation for my work as a medium.

Paul's mother and I talked endlessly about his short, but action-packed life. She worked hard to keep the memories of him alive, and would often say that she could feel his presence around her. I didn't doubt her. In fact, the more time I spent with her, the more I came to understand what she meant about his presence. At that time, it was extremely comforting, to feel as if Paul was watching over us.

Fate takes a hand

A short time later, whilst on my way home from work, I came across an advertisement in the local newspaper, which read in huge green letters: 'DORIS COLLINS, A WOMAN OF SPIRIT'. The article below explained that Doris was a Spiritualist medium and healer, and that she would be passing on messages from the other side and giving spiritual healing at the Odeon in Doncaster.

This was undoubtedly the first occasion when fate intervened in shaping my future. Here was a lady who believed that when we die our spirit is able to return and communicate with those we love through someone like herself – a medium. I was curious, especially as Paul's loss had led me to seriously question my own beliefs about life and death. I knew I had to find out more.

I telephoned Paul's mother and told her about the advertisement. I plucked up courage and asked if she would like to go and see if there were any messages from the other side for her. She jumped at the chance. I quickly cut the call short, and telephoned the Odeon. Much to my surprise, I managed to get the last two seats, although they were separate, which meant we would be unable to sit together. Instinctively I knew these tickets were to mark a turning point in my life.

Over the coming weeks, I continued to visit Paul's mother regularly to see how she was, and of course to chat about Paul and times gone by. Up to this point in my life, I had never thought about what happens when we die. Just like Tracy, I don't recall seeing spirit children when I was a child, nor did I have any strange dreams about 'ghosts' or spirits. I was, however, very sensitive and extremely intuitive – much to the annoyance of others.

For instance, at the age of 9 I confidently told my dad, 'Chloe, our cat, is going to have her five kittens tonight. I think I'll put her in the shed.'

The next morning, I got up and went straight outside to the coal shed. I was not the least bit surprised to find Chloe with her litter of kittens. I brought them inside in a box and put them in front of the fire. Then I noticed there were only four and I was convinced there should have been five!

I felt uneasy. I kept telling Mum there should be five kittens, but she just humoured me as parents often do. I was so unsettled that I decided to empty all the coal out of the shed. Mum was furious. I was covered in dust, and there was coal everywhere. She told me in no uncertain terms to get the mess cleaned up. I started throwing the coal back despondently. As I did so, I came across the fifth kitten that I'd known should be there, lying quite still, as if it was asleep. I gave the kitten a proper burial in the garden and placed a little cross over its grave.

Family ties

I was born in Lincolnshire, the youngest of four boys. My dad was in the Royal Air Force, stationed at Hemswell. From there we moved to Cranwell and then, when Dad left the forces, we moved to Kent to be near his mum. We settled in a village called Harvel.

We only lived there for a short time and then we moved to Northfleet, near Gravesend. I started school there and remember hating every minute of it. I was always in some kind of trouble and yet, despite disliking school, I did well in my lessons.

I was relatively happy at Northfleet until one day a bombshell was dropped: we were moving to Yorkshire to be nearer Mum's family. I was 10 at the time and I really didn't want to leave Kent.

We moved in September 1976 and all six of us squeezed into a small van for the long journey north to Doncaster. We arrived around midnight, and all crashed out on mattresses on the floor of our new home.

For some reason, I was really against starting another new school. Maybe I sensed I wouldn't fit in. I had a very southern accent and was nicknamed 'Kenty', and was inevitably picked on for being different.

Life went steadily downhill. I started skipping school, began smoking and hanging around with the wrong crowd. This culminated in me going into care. I blamed Mum for 'making us' move to this horrible place. I hated it. I didn't like the people – they obviously didn't like me – and I didn't like the house or the school. All I wanted was to go back to Kent where I had been happy. Several times I tried to do this. I attempted to catch the train to London, hitchhiked down the motorway, and even tried to get on a boat to Africa. Of course all this played havoc with my education and I never took any examinations.

After leaving school, I worked for a year on a Youth Opportunity Scheme with children who had special needs. Then I worked in a clothes shop, and eventually got a job at a DIY superstore. I became independent, earning my own money, and was free to do what I wanted.

In April 1984 I was interviewed for a position as a butler at Buckingham Palace. In May, I received a letter telling me I had been successful. I was overjoyed. Not only had I got the job, but more importantly I would be living in London (which was near Kent).

I started on 6 June 1984. That day, I saw the Queen and Prince Philip, Prince Charles and Princess Diana, Margaret Thatcher, Ronald and Nancy Reagan and many others returning to the Palace for a banquet marking the anniversary of the Normandy Landings.

A few days after I had started at the Palace, however, I was called to the personnel office. Apparently, I was supposed to have told the Palace that I had been in care as a child. I hadn't mentioned this because when I asked for advice, my social worker had told me that I didn't need to. The Palace accused me of lying to get the job and I was instantly dismissed. I was devastated; I'd given up a good job and left everything behind to work at the Palace. Everyone knew I'd gone to work there. How on earth could I tell people what had happened?

I spent the night walking the streets of London, feeling desperate and alone. I couldn't face going back to Doncaster, so I found the courage to telephone my nan, who lived in Meopham, Kent, and she said I could stay with her. She was really kind and understanding; she encouraged me to pick myself up and gave me the confidence to return home.

When I got back to Doncaster my first priority was to find a job. I managed to get taken on at a new nightclub called Seventh Heaven. It was whilst I was working there that Paul was killed, and I booked the tickets to see Doris Collins. Had I been working at Buckingham Palace at this time, I might not have seen the advertisements for Doris's event at the Odeon. And, looking back, I am certain my life would not have travelled in the direction it has done since.

Losing Dad

A few weeks before Doris's show, my dad had to go into hospital. He had been out of work for some time, and this, amongst other things, had caused him to become depressed.

Dad had only been in hospital for a couple of weeks when his doctor felt that he was much better and should come home. He himself didn't feel ready to leave at that stage, but with some encouragement from the nursing staff, reluctantly agreed. I didn't get to see much of him at that time because I was often out until the early hours of the morning working at Seventh Heaven and would spend most of the next day catching up on sleep.

On Easter Sunday 1985 I didn't have any change for my bus fare, so I asked Dad if he could lend me some until the following day. Being out of work, he had very little money, but I managed to charm him into parting with some of his cash. 'Here,' he said, with a grin. 'Thirty-six pence, and make sure you pay it back.'

'I promise,' I replied, as I went through the door.

Little did I realise this would be the last time I would see him alive.

After work that night some friends were going on to a party and they asked me along. During the evening, one of the bar staff, Mandy, produced a pack of Tarot cards.

I'd heard a bit about Tarot cards from friends at school, but I'd never had a reading myself. I immediately volunteered to go first.

I picked out some cards and gave them to Mandy.

She fixed her gaze between the cards and myself, then started talking quickly. 'There is a change at work, I see a different job.' I listened intently. 'You will have very little spare time. Your future is bright. You will have many children.' I wasn't convinced by what I was hearing.

She continued, 'There will be an upset at home very soon, I feel a–'

She frowned, and then stopped abruptly.

'What is it? What did you see?' I demanded.

'Nothing,' she said, innocently.

'Come on,' I urged. 'You must tell me – I'm getting worried.'

'There is going to be a death. Now, let's forget it. Who knows anyway? I'm probably wrong,' she snapped, as she got up and left the room.

I thought nothing more of the incident and got chatting to a group of friends. The party continued until about 4.30 a.m. and then everyone crashed out wherever they could find a comfortable place.

I'd been asleep for what I thought was just a couple of hours, when I looked at my watch and realised it was 3 in the afternoon. I stood up, made my way over the bodies lying around, and headed for the door. I had to be back at work for 7 p.m. that evening so I was in a hurry to get home.

I'd got about halfway when I started to feel a bit queasy. I stopped for a while to have a cigarette, which only made me feel worse, so I stubbed it out. My head was still pounding to the beat of the music from the party, and my stomach, by this time, really was heaving. Eventually I had to sit down. Almost immediately, a shudder ran down my spine and my head began to spin. Suddenly, out of nowhere, an image of Dad appeared in my mind. He was smiling. It was really strange, like looking at a photograph through a misted window. The picture stayed there for a few moments. I blinked a couple of times to try and clear it, but it remained.

Eventually I managed to pick myself up and started off home again. Despite feeling dizzy, I began to walk a lot more quickly. By the time I got there, I was out of breath. I stopped for a few seconds to compose myself, walked casually up the drive, opened the back door and went in. Mum was waiting for me.

The look on her face will remain with me for as long as I live.

'Where have you been, Paul?' she asked. Before I had a chance to reply, she went on, 'It's your dad …' She paused, obviously not quite sure how to continue. 'He's dead – he hung himself this morning. We've been trying to get hold of you all day.'

I felt my legs weaken beneath me and I reached for a chair; the rest is just a blur. Apparently, I went to work as usual that night, but I don't remember much about it. I think the adrenalin kicked in and got me through that terrible time.

I went to see Dad at the Chapel of Rest every day, to have a chat with him about work and life in general. Occasionally I would pause, as if waiting for him to respond in some way. I wanted to spend as much time with him as I possibly could.

The funeral was the worst part. There were just close family and friends present, and the service was taken by the same Salvation Army Officer who had taken Paul's funeral service. I felt angry inside because it didn't last very long and it seemed to me as if a whole life was discussed and then brushed aside in 20 minutes. People often say that out of bad can come good and, strangely enough, at Dad's funeral, I met my grandad for the first and only time in my life. Since his divorce from my nan he'd never made contact with us or his own children because he feared that someone would let her know where he lived.

After the funeral everyone went their own separate ways. This was the hardest part for me. While Dad had been at the Chapel of Rest, at least I had something to focus on, something to remember. Even during the funeral service, there was something there that we could see. Now, all that was left was memories. I couldn't, in fact *wouldn't*, accept things the way they were. There just had to be something else,

I was absolutely sure of it, but I just didn't know where to find it.

How strange that I had those two tickets to see Doris Collins tucked away in my wallet. Maybe she would be able to provide some answers? It was only a couple of weeks away now, and more than ever I felt the urge to go along, almost as if I was being guided there.

Finding hope

On the night there was a huge crowd outside the Odeon, and a great sense of excitement as we took our seats in the theatre. The house music was soon drowned out by the noise of the audience as they gathered together to see Doris work. I had a lovely warm feeling inside me, a feeling of calmness and peace, of being in exactly the right place, a place which would help me to understand my feelings about death. I glanced over to the other side of the balcony where Paul's mum was sitting, and she gave me a reassuring wave. We both had great expectations for this evening, and had pinned so many hopes on Doris, who was waiting in the wings.

The lights dimmed and the audience quietened. Without any warning, suddenly a voice boomed over the public address system: 'Ladies and gentlemen, would you please put your hands together and welcome – 'A Woman of Spirit – Doris Collins!'

We all joined together and loudly applauded Doris as she made her way to the centre of the stage.

In next to no time, she was picking out members of the audience, giving them pertinent information about their 'dead' loved ones. The messages brought a whole host of mixed reactions – both tears and laughter, as well as frequent gasps of amazement at what was being said. The atmosphere in the theatre that night was amazing. Soon it was time for Doris to finish the clairvoyance part of the show and to move on to the Spiritual healing.

Despite being disappointed at not receiving a message, Doris's show did make me feel considerably better – at least I now had hope. On the way out, I was handed a leaflet that gave details of a local Spiritualist church. Paul's mum had already visited such a place and she explained to me that it was very similar to the evening we had just attended, except that it was more religious, with hymns and prayers.

A few weeks passed while I tried to pluck up courage to visit the church mentioned in Doris Collins's leaflets. For some reason, I felt really scared, and when I finally found myself standing outside the ornate building, I had to take a deep breath before I could walk in. Just as Paul's mum had said, the inside appeared no different from any other church I had been in. On entering, I was given a hymn book by the lady at the door and directed to a seat. The room was nicely decorated, with a platform at one end.

The service began with a couple of hymns and prayers, but then the medium, an elderly gentleman, started to give out messages, just as Doris Collins had done at the Odeon.

Suddenly he pointed to me, and told me he had something to tell me.

'Who, me?' I stammered.

'Yes, you! You have a grandfather in the spirit world who passed over with chest trouble.'

As it happened, Mum's dad had passed away with a chest complaint, so I agreed, and the medium went on, 'He's telling me you have been brought here for a reason. You too are a medium. You will one day travel in this country and abroad, spreading the message that life is continuous, just as I do. You don't believe me, do you?'

'Er, well…' I mumbled.

By this time, most of the congregation was turning around and glaring at me, and my face was scarlet with embarrassment.

'Well, sonny,' he said, 'I am to give you one name which will be very important to you over the next two years of your life. You will remember it. This will prove to you that what we are saying is true, and one day soon you will be standing here on this spot, repeating what I have been telling you. The name I have to give you is *Gwyneth Williams.*'

I'd most certainly never heard of a lady with that name before, but I accepted the message out of politeness.

After the service had finished, I made a quick exit. On the way home, feeling somewhat disappointed that neither Dad nor Paul had come to speak, I repeated the message in my head. I still couldn't make head nor tail of it. However, I'd now overcome my initial nervousness about going to the Spiritualist church, so I decided that I would attend regularly. Perhaps in time my dad and Paul would be able to get a message through to me.

Joining the circle

Because I worked such odd hours, often I was only able to go to what the church called the 'Monday Night Open Circle'. This was quite a different meeting from the one held by Doris Collins at the Odeon and the service I had attended on my first visit to the church.

Instead of there being just one medium present, there were a few, all gathered in a large circle. The circle also included people who weren't mediums, who were hoping to receive a message. At each meeting I went to, I was told exactly the same thing – that I too would soon be working as a medium, travelling hundreds of miles and appearing in front of many people. Sadly, at that time, this was not what I wanted to hear. I just wanted to hear from my loved ones in the spirit world, and to know that they were OK.

Eventually, Edie, a lady I met there, was kind enough to take me under her wing. I discovered that she originally came from Kent, so I had an immediate affinity with her and we became very good friends. I confided in her about losing my dad and Paul, and told her about the feelings I'd had on my way home from the party before I knew Dad had died. Edie explained that he had obviously tried to get through to me himself to let me know he had passed away and that he was all right on the other side. I also told her about the messages I'd received, informing me that I was to be a medium myself.

As time passed, Edie taught me how to meditate and how to 'tune in', as she called it, so that I could talk with the spirit people myself. 'Just talk to them like you do anyone else,' she often said, 'and in time they will answer you.' I soon started to get the pictures in my mind, just as when I'd seen Dad immediately after his death.

Through Edie, I was able to understand the meaning of these pictures. She taught me how to use the 'third eye', as she called it, and how to interpret the images and feelings I had. Each week became a totally new experience, and my mind started to function in ways I never knew possible. I hadn't heard any voices or seen anything of substance, but Edie insisted that I was developing my gift gradually, at the right pace. She eventually suggested I join a mediums' teaching group, called a development circle, which she said would help me to allow my gift to unfold.

Edie then introduced me to two friends of hers, Sandy and Len Jones, who invited me to join their development group. Sandy told me it would be rather like going to a school where she, the teacher, would teach us, the pupils, how to receive spirit messages. The rest of it would then be up to us. She explained that she wouldn't be able to make it happen for us, but she would be able to show us the way. Both Sandy and Len emphasised the need for me to be punctual, interested, and above all, disciplined in my approach towards the group and any development that might take place.

Although I was still unsure, something inside urged me to join the group. Everything that had happened so far seemed to be leading up to this decision. And once it was made, my fate was sealed.

CHAPTER 3
Tracy: There's no such thing as ghosts!

In the 1980s, when Paul was working at Seventh Heaven in Doncaster, I used to go there regularly with friends. I had just started working in my local Unemployment Benefit Office as a clerical officer, and was really proud of my new job. However, because Retford is such a small town, everyone seems to know everyone else. If we went out locally we were often accosted by people wanting to know why they hadn't received their giro that week! So it made sense to go to a club in Doncaster instead.

I often wonder what would have happened if I had got chatting to Paul on one of my regular nights out at Seventh Heaven. Would we have become friends then? Or did we need to travel different paths for a while to make it more meaningful when we did eventually find each other? It certainly makes us smile when we think about the fact that we could have met up many years before we did.

Like Paul, my first experience of mediumship came during my teenage years. Paul chose to seek out information about Spiritualism because he had lost people close to him, and he needed the comfort of knowing those people were still around. My own introduction to mediumship came in a very roundabout way, however, through my mum's interest in the supernatural.

To believe, or not to believe?

I was the eldest of four children; I had two brothers, Adrian and Nigel, and a sister, Lisa. We lived in a council house in the centre of Retford, and both my parents worked. As a child, I spent a lot of time with Nana and Grandad Carter, who lived over the road. I enjoyed my own company, and always had my head in a book. Mum had developed an interest in spiritualism after she lost a baby five months into the pregnancy, and she often went out in the evenings to see mediums. I didn't really know much about any of this – and in all honesty, when I think back, I didn't *want* to know. Whenever Mum tried to tell the family about her experiences we paid very little attention and humoured her for a short while before finding other things to do with our time. I actually remember thinking to myself that she was a bit weird – after all, there are no such things as ghosts, are there? At that time, I couldn't possibly conceive that there could be a spirit world. I suppose I treated Mum's evenings out as a bit of a joke, and got on with the more important task of being a teenager in the 1980s.

One night, I was doing my homework in my bedroom when Mum came up to the room I shared with Lisa. I was fully prepared for a telling-off about the disgusting pile of clothes I had left all over the floor, and so, in typical teenage fashion, I completely ignored her as she stood in the doorway, watching me. My mum is only a little lady in height, but she has a big personality. As I looked up I noticed her short dark hair was perfect, as was her make-up, and she'd got her best clothes on.

'If you're fed up, why don't you come with me?' she offered. 'I've got a reading booked with a medium at Gladys's.'

With this, she turned round and went into her own bedroom to spray on a bit of her favourite perfume, and to put on her coat. I was somewhat surprised to receive such an invitation but secretly excited to be chosen out of the four of us to go with her.

It took us about ten minutes to walk round to Gladys's. I remember asking her a few questions about what was going to happen when we got there. I can't remember her answers, but they obviously did nothing to reassure me, for as we got nearer to the house, I remember beginning to feel quite nervous. What if there were such things as ghosts, after all? What if I saw one? What if I became possessed? A whole host of strange thoughts went through my mind, and I felt very scared as we entered the house and were ushered into the front room.

Whatever I expected, it wasn't the sight that met me there. There were about ten women in the room. The wine was flowing freely, and the atmosphere was merry, with much laughter. This didn't quite match the images I had seen on TV of little old ladies sitting around a table with their hands joined, asking, 'Is there anybody there?'

'Come in, Janice, and you, Trace, come and sit down. What do you want to drink?' Gladys fussed around us, finding us seats, fetching us drinks. It was very noisy, everyone talking amongst themselves – and every now and then one of the women would leave the room to go next door and see the medium.

Eventually it was Mum's turn to go for her reading. I felt extremely uncomfortable as she left the room, and slightly protective towards her. Even though the women who had been in to see the medium previously were all coming back to the lounge marvelling at the things they had been told, I was still feeling a little sceptical about the whole scenario, and I had a horrible feeling Mum was about to be conned.

After about half an hour, she returned to the lounge, and I noticed she had tears running down her cheeks. The other women gathered around her, and she told them that my grandad Charlie had come through to speak to her. She was overjoyed with the message she had received.

Soon afterwards, we left. We didn't say very much on the way home. I didn't ask her about the message she had received, and she didn't volunteer any information.

It had been an interesting experience, but not a convincing one for me. I still did not believe in the possibility of life after death, as I had not experienced anything first-hand that led me to accept there was such a thing. It was scary to think that dead people could come and talk to us, and I didn't really welcome the idea.

An early encounter

I rarely thought of that evening afterwards, nor did I pay much attention to Mum's interest in the after-life. She continued to visit mediums throughout my teenage years and eventually decided to open her own Spiritualist church, where she remained President for a number of years. Every Saturday evening, she would open up her little hall, and welcome in an audience of around 50 people. Afterwards, she would run her own open circle and people came from miles around to sit with her and receive messages.

Mum has suffered many tragedies over the years, and I know that Spiritualism has helped her to overcome her losses, and has given her a purpose in life. She tells many interesting stories about mediums she has seen, and messages she has received. Her favourite story, which she tells to this day, is of a message she received from a young man whose work as a medium was taking the area by storm, and who she was lucky enough to see at Retford Town Hall.

The medium was looking for a person in the audience who could understand the surname Marshall. Even though this name was significant to my mum, she did not put her hand up. The medium spoke of a father-in-law in the spirit world who had passed over following stomach cancer. This information corresponded with my mum's father-in-law, but still she didn't speak up. The medium continued, telling the audience that whoever he wanted to speak to had taken twenty pounds out of the cash machine on Grove Street – but that the money had come from an account which didn't belong to them. Eventually, the medium pointed directly to Mum, and said, 'Madam, I feel drawn to you. Have you taken twenty pounds out of your husband's bank account before coming here this evening?' Reluctantly, my mum agreed that yes, she had, and yes, she could understand the surname Marshall, and the father-in-law who was trying to communicate. The audience was in hysterics – particularly a group of women two rows back from my mum, who all worked with my dad at a local factory in Retford.

The medium proceeded with his message, and to the delight of the audience told her that this wasn't the first time she had 'borrowed' money from her husband's bank account.

My mum still giggles about this incident, saying it shows how you can never have any secrets from the spirit world. She also maintains that the medium who gave her this message is the best she's ever seen, and that over the years he has given her outstanding proof of life after death. That medium was Paul Norton! My mum knew Paul for many years before I met him – another strange twist of fate that meant we could have met up sooner than we did.

Highs and lows

Around the time that Paul was starting to work regularly as a medium, I was leading a very different life. After leaving school I had attended college for a while, completed a couple of Youth Training Schemes and then managed to secure employment in the Civil Service at the Unemployment Benefit Office in Retford. I got married when I was 20 years old; my husband was a year younger than me at 19 and he worked in a local factory. We bought a brand new semi-detached house near where my mum lived, and I felt happy and content with life – even more so, when I found I was pregnant, just two months after getting married. Sadly, my happiness was very short-lived. Three months into the pregnancy, I was advised that my baby had died inside me and would have to be removed.

Following the loss of this baby, my mood altered, and I spent many hours contemplating my loss. I found it very difficult to come to terms with the fact that the baby that had been alive and growing inside me was no longer there, and no longer a part of my life. Until this point, I had never really experienced a personal bereavement. My grandad Charlie (my dad's dad) had died when I was about 11 years old, but I had not known him that well, and had not mourned his loss as I now mourned this child.

Because my mood was low, my husband organised a holiday in Corfu to cheer me up and give me something to look forward to. We had a wonderful time, even though 1986 was the year when people were dropping dead in the streets in Greece because of the extreme heat. As we flew out of Corfu to return home, planes were scooping water from the sea to pour onto forest fires, which were raging in the lush countryside. I remember feeling very ill on returning home, but put my lethargy and nausea down to the effects of too much wine, food and the overwhelming heat we had experienced whilst abroad. It was only when I had been vomiting every morning for a week that I began to suspect I might be pregnant again. I booked myself an appointment with my GP, who confirmed that I was around two months' pregnant. I was advised to rest, and because of my earlier miscarriage, was given an urgent appointment at the ante-natal clinic at Doncaster Royal Infirmary.

For some reason, I really did not want to go to the hospital that day. I had spoken to my mum on the phone before leaving the house, and had cried pitifully, telling her I didn't want to go. Although she had reassured me that all would be well, I wasn't convinced, and a sense of pain hung over me. I had to go on my own as my husband was working. I was only kept waiting a short time when I arrived at the hospital, and when I saw the consultant he said he wanted me to have a scan before he examined me further. I was encouraged to drink pints of water and then sit in a corridor with several other women, who were also waiting for scans.

The nurse began the procedure, placing the cold gel on my skin and then running the scanning device all over my stomach in order to pick up an image of the baby. At this point the screen was pointed towards me. However, after a few minutes, the screen was turned away from me, and I was asked to get dressed and remain in a small waiting room just down the corridor. I knew something was wrong – why else would I not have been allowed to see my baby? I sat in the waiting room and began to prepare for the worst. As I waited for the consultant, somehow, I felt numb and alone. I knew what he was going to say.

I remember the consultant taking my hand and gently advising me that this baby had died about two weeks ago – they could tell this by the measurements they had taken from the scan. I had been carrying a dead baby around inside me all that time. I felt abnormal: what was wrong with me? Why couldn't my babies grow normally inside me like other women's?

An appointment was made for me to be admitted to hospital the following week, and I left to catch the bus home. When I got in, I telephoned my husband and he came home from work. We coped with our grief by putting our energy into thinking about the wedding we had been invited to that weekend.

Another sad loss

It was going to be difficult facing family and friends, but I knew I had to be strong and get through the day. Little did I realise that I would need to be even stronger than I had anticipated.

I was just getting ready when, at eleven o'clock on the day of the wedding, the telephone rang.

It was my brother Adrian. 'Hi, Sis,' he said quietly. I could tell by the tone of his voice that this was going to be bad news.

'What's up?' I asked immediately.

'Nana Jackson was found dead this morning. The police are there – they have to check out the circumstances because she was found on the floor.'

My immediate thoughts were for my dad. He would be devastated at the loss of his mother, to whom he was extremely close. 'How's Dad?' I asked.

'Not so good,' Adrian replied. 'I don't know if he'll be at the wedding this afternoon.'

'Is there anything I can do to help?' I asked.

'Not really. Dad's down at the house now. I'll see you at the church – we can talk there,' and then he was gone.

I put down the phone and went to sit on the bed. Suddenly I felt surrounded by death. The fact that we only have a short time to live became all too real. I had not been particularly close to my Nana Jackson but it was so sad to think of her dying in this way. I now had two losses to cope with, and knew I was going to find the wedding even more difficult.

People were very kind when we arrived at the church,

tactfully enquiring about my health, and asking how Dad was. I could only reply that I didn't know, as I hadn't spoken to him. We waited outside the church, and just before it was time to go inside for the ceremony, a taxi arrived and my mum and dad got out. I felt an overwhelming desire to rush up and put my arms around my dad, but he wouldn't have appreciated this under the circumstances, and so I quietly waited for him to approach me. His shoulders were stooped, his head bowed, and his skin was grey. I asked him if he was all right.

'I'm fine, Trace,' he said, but the tears in his eyes told me otherwise. He scrunched up his eyes, and held his hands to his face. Thankfully everyone else there had the sensitivity to leave us to this private moment.

I felt humbled to be in my dad's presence at this time. I had been selfishly engrossed in my feelings of grief for a baby who had not yet been born, when this man standing in front of me had just lost his mother – the person who had brought him up and cared for him, taught him valuable lessons in life, and supported him in times of need. I could not even begin to comprehend how he was feeling.

How I wanted to bring her back for him, to make her alive again so that all his pain could stop! I am sure this was the first stirring of the need within me to help others by reuniting them with their loved ones in the spirit world. We eventually went into the church, and the wedding took place. My dad came to the reception, but left after a short while, his need to be alone with his grief quite apparent.

On the following Monday I went into hospital for the operation to remove my baby. I was now resigned to the fact that he was dead, and needed to be taken away to prevent infection. The operation went well, and I was sitting up in bed when my husband came to visit me in the evening.

The saddest thing about the gynaecological wards at that time was that they backed onto the maternity wing, and the cries of new babies echoed around the corridors. I found this difficult to cope with and wanted to go home. I begged my husband to allow me to discharge myself, as the sound of the babies crying was making me want to scream, so I signed the necessary paperwork and got dressed. I was so weak, my husband literally carried me down the corridor, and out to the car.

A joyful meeting

I spent the next couple of days in bed, drifting in and out of consciousness. I was really drained. My husband was working 12-hour shifts at the time, and came and went without disturbing me. Poor man, he really had to fend for himself as I was in no fit state to look after him.

On the third morning I awoke with sunlight streaming through the bedroom window. The room was hot and stuffy, so I flung the covers off and turned over in bed. I couldn't get comfortable; my back was aching so I turned around to face the windows again. Suddenly I felt a strange sense of peace settle about the room, and my feelings of depression and the pain in my body disappeared. I opened my eyes, and standing there, with the sunlight behind her, was my Nana Jackson. This can't be real, I thought, Nana Jackson is dead – she died on Saturday.

As I looked towards her, she moved closer to the bed. She looked radiant, a beautiful luminous glow settling around her. Her grey hair shone white in the sunlight, her skin was a rosy pink, and her eyes twinkled merrily from behind her glasses. She looked years younger than she had appeared the last time I had seen her when she was alive; at my wedding the previous December. She smiled at me – a beautiful smile that lit up her whole face. As she leaned closer to me, I felt overjoyed. I had the sensation of her taking my hand, and placing a light kiss upon my forehead.

Then, sadly, she disappeared, just as quickly as she had arrived. I was overwhelmed with sorrow that she was no longer there. But after she had gone, my physical pain subsided, and for the first time in three days, I wanted to get up and go about my normal daily business. I had a bath, did my hair and make-up, and set about washing the pots and doing a spot of light housework. When my husband returned from work, he seemed pleased to see me up and about and feeling better. After we had eaten, and settled down in front of the telly, I couldn't wait to tell him about the experience I had had in the morning, when I was convinced my dead grandmother had been to see me.

I told my husband in great detail about what I had seen, and how I had felt. He wasn't particularly interested and said it must have been a dream. I agreed that he was probably right. However, deep down inside, I knew something special had occurred. Somehow my grandmother had found a way to come back and show me that she lived on – maybe in a different place – but she was alive, I was certain of it.

I felt I had to repay her in some way, and so I offered to

help out at the funeral with the catering. I knew this would make my dad happy as well. On the actual day I remained at my parents' house, preparing sandwiches and cutting cake, getting everything ready for the family members who would soon be returning to the house to mourn together. When the family came in, the sense of grief hung heavily in the air. I wanted to share with them the knowledge that Nana was all right, that she was still alive, that she had shown herself to me – but of course I didn't. Day by day, the need within me to bring comfort to others was growing stronger. Something was changing inside me, and I yearned to reach out and touch people, to help them in their hour of need, just as I had been helped by the spirit of my nana. However, I would not discover my ability as a medium until a couple of years later. So, for the time being, I put all thoughts of death aside.

Like most 21-year-olds, I was very busy. I worked hard at my job, and soon I was in line for promotion. Life was beginning to feel good again.

My first child was born in October 1988 – a bonny 10lb 4oz baby girl. I named her Gemma, as she was certainly a little gem to me. She was born in Doncaster, where Paul lived, and where he was well known locally as an excellent medium. Everyone joked that she would be able to play cricket for Yorkshire when she grew up.

I had had a difficult pregnancy, needing hormone injections in my spine for most of the nine months to ensure my baby would live. Throughout this time, I was very aware of Nana Jackson being around me. I dreamed of her often, and sensed her presence at home. Somehow, whenever I felt her close, I was overwhelmed by a sense of peace and security. When I didn't feel her close, I tried to hold these feelings within me, to keep me going. During the birth, I quite clearly saw her standing to one side of the bed. She had the same luminous quality about her that I had seen that day in my bedroom. Knowing she was there gave me the strength and courage to deliver my beautiful baby.

My mum also acknowledges that Nana Jackson has been to see her on several occasions – usually in times of difficulty, to help soothe and restore calm. The spirit people have a wonderful ability to do this – to enter our lives when we most need them, and to bring peace and harmony.

Nana Jackson was the first spirit person I was aware of seeing. I'm so pleased that it was she who was chosen to help me in this way – to open my eyes to the possibility of life after death, and to make me want to find out more.

CHAPTER 4
Paul: 'Drawing the short straw'

When we first met, Tracy and I were amazed at the number of coincidences there were in our lives. We lived only 20 miles apart, and our paths had crossed so many times, yet amazingly we had never met.

In the 1980s, Tracy often came to the nightclub where I worked, but I don't recall ever seeing her there and she doesn't remember me. When I first started working as a medium I met Janice, Tracy's mum, many times, but never knew she had children. Looking back, we can now only assume that the spirit world was waiting for the right time to bring us together. As you read about our lives, you will see that, although I am only one year older than Tracy, and we grew up in the same era, we held very different views on life, and death.

I was already a believer in the possibility of 'life after death'. Maybe this was because I had had more experience of losing loved ones, or maybe I was just more inquisitive and open-minded. I knew I had to find out more, and learn about the spirit world for myself. Once the idea of sitting in Sandy's teaching group had been put to me, I became more enthusiastic, and couldn't wait for the first meeting.

The adventure begins

The bus journey was long enough for me to think about this new adventure in my life, and I was feeling both nervous and excited. I could see Len standing in the doorway as I drew near the house.

'We thought you'd changed your mind,' he shouted out, loud enough for the whole street to hear. Part of me wished I had! The rest of the group had already arrived and Sandy introduced me to them in turn.

'This is Gary,' she said, 'Pauline, Rosemary, David, Carol, and Lillian.'

I looked around; they all appeared keen to catch a glimpse of the 'new boy'. 'You can sit there, Paul,' Sandy offered, pointing to a chair in the corner.

When we were all finally seated and relaxed, Sandy turned down the lights, said a little prayer and then told us we were going to meditate. She asked us to follow what she was saying in our minds whilst she took us on a guided 'walk' through countryside, which we had to visualise.

'I'm going to leave you all now for a while,' she said, 'so that you can find some inner peace.'

I drifted off quite happily, my tired mind filled with thoughts of the beautiful place that Sandy had described. I pictured myself in a magical woodland clearing, with magnificent silver birch trees all around me. I sat on a log, and basked in the glorious sunlight as butterflies landed on my arms, and birds sat on my shoulders. The images I saw were so lifelike, and I even thought I could feel a breeze on my face. The next 45 minutes passed really quickly.

Sandy spoke again. 'Now,' she said, 'in your own time, I want you to come back to the group and open your eyes.'

I'd relaxed my mind so much that I could have gone to sleep right there and then. I couldn't remember the last time I'd felt so good inside. Sandy asked each of us what, if anything, we had seen or heard. Everyone else's stories seemed so grand. They spoke of seeing and hearing people, vast spaces and colours, and marvellous music. Yet mine were so ordinary.

'I just pictured what you were describing, Sandy,' I said, somewhat uncomfortably. Sandy paused for a moment.

'You've done well for your first time, Paul,' she replied, with an air of confidence. The others seemed to agree.

Becoming a student

Despite feeling disappointed that I hadn't experienced anything extraordinary, I really did enjoy the meeting and I was convinced that the results would come in time.

Afterwards, Sandy and Len invited both Pauline and me to stay behind. We had a long chat and Sandy explained what the spirit world was like, and how mediums worked. Before I left, she gave me a book to read about psychic development and told me to be open-minded about the different ways that it described.

Pauline lived only a couple of miles away from me, and kindly offered to give me a lift home and pick me up the following week. I readily accepted. I'd been so used to relying on public transport, or my legs, that being offered a lift was a luxury.

That evening, I decided to read Sandy's book. It described various exercises that students could follow to help enhance their psychic powers. I decided to try some of them out, but had very little success.

Over the next week, I worked my way through most of the exercises and started to become despondent when things didn't go to plan. During that same week I was due to start my new college course so naturally my thoughts turned to this instead.

I was taking a full-time two-year course in Social Care at High Melton College, Doncaster. Each term, the students would be going to different residential homes and schools to gain some 'hands on' experience, as well as studying the theory of social care at college.

A memorable name

High Melton is a beautiful little village and the college was an ideal place for people to learn. There is an old church in the grounds and some of the college buildings are quite an age too. The site is on a hill and there are acres of trees and fields surrounding it. I fell in love with the place the minute I set eyes on it.

I had the admission letter with me; it gave instructions on how to find the main lecture room that we would be using. We were to meet in room GW2, below the library, at 9 a.m. I asked someone for directions and made my way across the site. I was just admiring the view when a cold shudder went down my spine, and the hairs on my arms began to stand on end. As I looked up towards the library, written across the front in huge bold letters was the name 'GWYNETH WILLIAMS'.

Almost immediately, the words came flooding back.

'*I have to give you the name Gwyneth Williams.*'

It was the name the medium had given me the first time I'd gone to the Spiritualist church. He had also told me that this name would be very important to me for the next two years and that it would confirm his message was true. I was dumbfounded that the name was not only correct, but manifested itself at the same time as I was starting to learn about mediumship.

I finally realised that the medium had told me the truth, and I couldn't wait to get to the next teaching group to share my news.

Sandy said that she knew exactly what the spirit world was doing, and that I was to wait and see what they had in store for me, as it was my destiny.

We then had another meditation. This time Sandy asked us to visualise a beach, where we were greeted by a couple of dolphins that took us far out into the sea, and then beneath the surface. Once again, Sandy left us with our own thoughts for about 40 minutes.

Afterwards the others impressed me with their accounts of what they had seen during the meditation. Once again I didn't feel I had experienced anything other than a peaceful sensation. I couldn't help feeling disappointed, particularly after what had taken place that week. Sandy could obviously sense this and she took me to one side and suggested that I meditate each day for half an hour over the next week. She told me that this would definitely help. I believed her and decided that I would do just as she had suggested.

The mist begins to clear

The following day when I got home from college, I went straight to my bedroom, closed the curtains, put on some classical music and started to meditate just as Sandy had advised. I didn't think of anything in particular, but I did notice a multitude of colours in my mind. As the colours swirled around in my head, I started to feel quite drowsy, almost as if I was being hypnotised, and to my annoyance I fell asleep.

This happened every time I meditated for about five weeks. Then one night I began to meditate and as usual the colours were soon apparent within my mind. The overwhelming feeling of drowsiness, which was now so familiar, started to overcome me. However, this night there was a significant difference.

After a few moments of basking in the colours, I began to feel aware of a change in the atmosphere and thought I could sense another presence in the room. I felt as though I knew who the person was, but I didn't dare open my eyes.

'Mum, is that you?' I asked. There was no response. 'Steven, Gary, Tony?' Again there was no reply. In fact, there wasn't a single sound within the room; yet I was absolutely sure there was someone there. This was confirmed when I heard someone speak.

'I am Naiomi,' said the gentle voice. I froze for a moment in disbelief.

'I am your guide,' she continued. 'I work with others who want to help you. We've been waiting for you to come to us.

We have tried so hard to get through to you, but you filled your mind with books,' she said.

'I have come to tell you that all you have been told is true, and that it is time for you to start your work.'

I didn't know what to say.

'There is something more you should know,' she added. 'We will be with you on the third. You must have trust in what we say, and then you will see how we will be working together.' And with this statement, the voice slowly faded away, and I no longer felt the presence within the room.

I was totally confused and amazed.

The short straw

For the next few days I was in a bit of a daze. My mind kept replaying the incident as I tried to make sense of what had happened.

At the next teaching group, I told everyone what I had experienced. They appeared to be just as amazed as I had been.

'She told me that they would be with me on the third,' I repeated. Before I had a chance to discuss what Naiomi could possibly have meant by this, Sandy interrupted the conversation.

'I have a tin here,' she said. 'There are seven straws in it. One of them is very small. Whoever picks this straw will be taking the service with me at Mexborough Spiritualist church next Sunday.' We all looked at each other in disbelief as Sandy passed the tin around. Just as it was being passed to me, I felt a little skip of my heart, and then came Naiomi's voice again, loud and clear in my mind.

'It's you, Paul, but remember what I told you,' I distinctly heard her say.

'Paul?' said Pauline, frowning a little. 'Are you all right?'

'Fine,' I replied.

Pauline chuckled. 'You don't look fine,' she said. 'In fact you look like you've just seen a ghost!'

'No!' I replied, 'I haven't *seen* one, but I just *heard* one.' This brought a serious look to her face.

'The guide I told you about earlier has just spoken to me again,' I whispered. 'She said it will be me who picks the shortest straw, and that I am to remember what she told me.'

At this point, Sandy placed the tin containing the straws in front of me. I looked her straight in the eye as I dipped my hand in, and pulled out a straw. She smiled at me with a knowing look. Sure enough, as I had been told by Naiomi, I had picked the shortest straw.

'Well, that settles it then,' Sandy said, looking quite amused.

Afterwards, she told me that she had already known I would be taking the service with her. She explained that that was why she had stopped me in mid-conversation. She reminded me that the date of the service was the 3 November! I later discovered that this was Edie's birthday, the lady who had encouraged me with my gifts, and introduced me to Sandy and Len. Strange forces seemed to be at work. Surely these were more than just coincidences?

I was filled with trepidation, but because I was so busy with my college work I didn't get much time to think about my debut as a medium the following Sunday.

First night nerves

The big day soon arrived and Sandy and Len arrived promptly at 5 p.m. to take me to the Spiritualist church in Mexborough in their car.

Upon entering the building we were immediately ushered into an ante-room. It was very small and crammed with old furniture. At this point my stomach started to heave and I felt as if I was on a rollercoaster. I looked at Sandy for reassurance, but all she could manage was a strained smile – she was obviously nervous herself. At least I'm not on my own, I thought. After only a few minutes, there came a faint knock at the door.

'Are you ready, my dears?' asked a kindly lady, who then led us into the main hall and onto the platform.

I knew that Sandy was a popular medium, but I never expected to see so many in the church. It was so packed that people were standing up at the back and in the aisles. After the initial introductions, hymns and prayers, Sandy gave a talk on the religion of Spiritualism, after which she gave some wonderful messages.

Then, suddenly, without any warning whatsoever, she stopped working and promptly announced that I would be continuing the service, after which she returned to her seat.

All I can remember of that night was the churning in my stomach and my legs feeling as if they were about to give way when I stood up in front of the congregation to speak. The rest of what happened is a complete blank.

Afterwards a small group of people gathered around me and

started to compliment me and shake my hand. I just smiled, thanked them, and moved over to where Sandy was seated.

'You did well, Paul,' she said. 'I'm so proud of you.'

The church officials must have agreed, because I was offered further bookings there and some people asked me if I would take services at a couple of the other churches in the area. Others asked if I did private meetings. I politely explained that I was at college full-time, and so, at that point, I didn't really have the time to do them.

'I'll get you some bookings of your own, Paul,' Sandy said, on the way home. I smiled in agreement, even though I wasn't sure if I was ready to take any more services just yet.

That evening, just before I went to sleep, I closed my eyes and said a little prayer of thanks to whoever had been responsible for helping me. I was just enjoying those few minutes' peace when my guide Naiomi whispered gently to me, 'I told you that we would help. You did well because you trusted. I will speak again with you soon.' And then she was gone.

Always remain humble

The following week, the main topic of conversation at Sandy's was the service we had taken. Some of the other members of the circle had been in the congregation.

It transpired that one of them knew one of the ladies I'd given a message to. It turned out that this lady had lost her husband in a fire. I'd apparently told her about this, given her his name and the date that he'd passed over, along with a short comforting message.

I'd had no idea what had taken place during the service and

this was valuable feedback about my capabilities as a medium. By this time, I was of course feeling quite pleased with myself; however, Sandy was quick to intervene.

'Always, Paul,' she said, 'you must remain humble!' I promised her that I certainly would.

'We're running late,' she added quickly, whilst switching on the cassette-player to begin the meditation. With all the chat about the service, we'd forgotten about starting the teaching. Sandy was always very particular about timing.

'We have made an agreement with the spirit world,' she would often remind us, adding, 'How would you like it if they were late to help you with a service or a one-to-one sitting?'

The group carried on meeting until Christmas, and then there was a break for the holiday. During this time, I decided to catch up with my college work and to concentrate on my own personal meditations.

During those holidays I thought about many things. I recalled all that had happened in my short life and, for the first time, it seemed as if everything was starting to fit into place. I realised that I owed a great deal to Edie, Sandy and Len. Without their help, I wouldn't have been able to achieve half of what I already had. At last I was starting to feel a sense of purpose. I had a goal to work towards: something very special that was close to my heart.

A terrible shock

The holidays were soon over, and it was back to college for me. The teaching group started up again and I was really pleased, as I had missed everyone during the break.

For me, Sandy's group was like an extended family, and this created a secure feeling for us all, enabling us to progress well with our development. Life seemed to be going well for me.

Then, quite unexpectedly, one Sunday afternoon, shortly after Christmas, I was at home, flicking through the pages of a magazine, when there was a knock at the door. I went to see who it was; I was surprised to see Janice, our next-door neighbour, standing there.

'Will you tell your mother that Phillip is on the phone for her?' (We didn't have a telephone of our own at the time, so Janice didn't mind people having her number in case there was an emergency.) Uncle Phillip is Dad's brother. He lived in Essex at the time. I passed the message on to Mum, and she rushed next door to take the call. I went back to my magazine, when suddenly Naiomi's voice interrupted my thoughts.

'It's not good news,' she said. 'Be prepared for the worst, but please realise that we are helping her.'

I wasn't sure what Naiomi was trying to tell me, and felt slightly confused. Just as I was about to ask for more information, Mum came back into the room looking extremely pale.

'It's your nan,' she said, swallowing deeply before continuing, 'She died on Friday; Phillip was phoning to let us know in case we saw it on the news.'

I didn't understand.

'News?' I questioned, in a state of shock.

'Your nan's been murdered,' came Mum's reply.

I felt physically sick and ran to the bathroom. Nan had been so good to me when I lost my job at the Palace and had got me right back on track with my life, encouraging me to return home to my family and find a job. I couldn't believe this was happening – surely it must be a bad dream?

First Paul had died, then Dad and now Nan, all within 14 months. My thoughts were in complete turmoil. Again it seemed as if my life was in bits.

Looking back, I think the reason I felt so bad was that each of these special people in my life had passed over to the spirit world in such a tragic and traumatic way. Maybe if they'd been ill, or if I'd had some warning that they were about to pass, I could have accepted their deaths more easily.

Even more bad news

Unbelievably, our grief wasn't to end there! Exactly one week later, we received another urgent telephone call from Phillip. This time, he had the sad duty of informing us that his father (my grandad) had also passed away.

Apparently, he'd been suffering from cancer for some time. As I mentioned earlier, the first and only time I'd ever met my grandad was at Dad's funeral, and I now felt extremely sad that we hadn't had the chance to get to know him better. Unfortunately, I suppose these kinds of thoughts always go through our minds when it's too late.

Finally, just one month later, Mum got a letter from Australia imparting the news that one of her aunties had also sadly passed away. She too had been suffering from cancer. Within a 14-month period, five people, one of whom was a family friend (but who was nevertheless still very close and important), had passed away, three of them in unusually tragic circumstances. It took quite some time for my family to overcome our grief, and to come to terms with all these sad losses.

Being able to communicate with the spirit world didn't make it any easier for me. I still missed the physical presence of all the people who had passed over, and craved the opportunity to pick up a phone and talk to them, or the chance to see them all just one more time.

What my involvement in spiritualism did do, though, was to help me to understand how other people felt during the grieving process, and this knowledge would be invaluable to me in my future work as a medium. I also took comfort from knowing that one day I would be reunited with my friends and family in the spirit world, and that the next time we came together it would be for eternity.

The murder of my grandmother was especially upsetting. As it transpired, the person who had murdered her had been doing some odd jobs for her at her home. Poor Nan! Although she had trusted this young man initially, she'd apparently discovered that he had been stealing money from her. When she confronted him, he offered to pay her back. However, on the day in question, he had returned to her house and, following some kind of disagreement, he had struck her a vicious blow to the head, killing her instantly. It wasn't until the early hours of the next morning that her body was discovered by a neighbour, who had seen smoke and flames coming from Nan's kitchen. This was as a result of several fires, which had been deliberately started around Nan's home.

The young man responsible was charged with manslaughter and was subsequently admitted to a secure mental hospital for a period of 18 months, but only served six. I felt angry and cheated – on two counts. Firstly, it was such a waste, because Nan's life had been taken away through no fault of her own. Secondly, a very troubled 18-year-old lad had been locked up for committing the crime. I felt sorry for him because he now had to face his whole life knowing what he'd done, as well as the difficult prospect of trying to integrate himself back into society, and finding a job after his release. After all, people were bound to find out what he had done.

Eventually, our lives slowly started to get back to some kind of normality. However, I still felt extremely sad about all that had happened, especially as I had intended to visit Nan in Meopham during the upcoming summer holidays. I had always looked forward to returning to that part of the country, but now that would never happen.

Just when I thought things couldn't get any worse, Sandy announced that she was closing the teaching group. I was extremely sad, as it had in some ways been a lifeline to me during this period.

On a more positive note, word had got around about the service I'd taken with Sandy at Mexborough and bookings at other churches had started to flood in. Although I was apprehensive and nervous at first, I had accepted them. I still had a few months to spare before I had to take my first service alone, so I decided to pay a visit to my good friend Edie and to start going back to the 'open circle' at church to get some much-needed practice. When I first joined Sandy's group, I had been so busy (with starting college, learning to meditate and coping with my grief) that I hadn't had any time left for going to church. To be honest, I had completely forgotten about it.

No longer having the opportunity to practise my newfound skills at Sandy's left me at a bit of a loose end. I thought that returning to my roots and going back to church would stand me in good stead for my forthcoming bookings as a medium, and would help to keep my thoughts occupied and focused.

CHAPTER 5
Tracy: A haunting time

I answered the phone as soon as it started to ring.

'Mrs Hall?' asked the estate agent.

'Yes,' I replied, eagerly.

'I'm pleased to let you know that we've had an offer on your property – it's the full asking price.'

'We'll accept,' I blurted out.

I was really excited. The birth of my daughter Gemma had made me realise that our two-bedroom semi was no longer large enough to accommodate us and all the paraphernalia that comes with a new baby. I began to get itchy feet, and decided I wanted to move. Eventually I managed to persuade my husband, and he reluctantly agreed to put the house up for sale.

We were very surprised when the house sold during the first weekend it was on the market. We spent the next week trailing around properties in Retford looking for our 'dream home'. I had a very fixed idea of what I wanted. I felt we needed something much larger – maybe with three bedrooms. I also yearned for another reception room downstairs, which could double as a dining room/sitting room for us, and a play-room for Gemma. I enjoyed entertaining friends and family, and so wherever we moved to needed to be large enough for family gatherings and dinner parties. My husband knew that I wouldn't settle for anything less!

None of the newer properties we looked at came anywhere close to meeting my criteria. Halfway through the week we decided to widen our search to include some older properties and I noticed a three-bedroomed Victorian terraced house, just round the corner from where we currently lived, and also only a couple of minutes' walk from my mum's. It was important that we find something close to her, as she was kindly looking after Gemma for us whilst I went out to work part-time. I was still working at the local Unemployment Benefit Office, and my job was going really well. We arranged to go and view the property on Saturday morning at eleven o'clock.

I fell in love with it the minute we walked through the door. It had everything we were looking for, and I saw it as a particularly good omen that there were some lily of the valley (Nana Carter's favourite flowers) growing in one corner of the neat front garden.

Inside, the house needed a lot of work. The current owners had started by renovating the kitchen, bathroom and second sitting room, but they wanted to move to something newer. They had lived there only a year. Further discussion revealed that the owners prior to them had only stayed six months. None of this, however, put me off. I had fallen in love with that house, and would have done anything to get my hands on it. Luckily, my husband felt the same, and so, immediately after the viewing, we went into the estate agent's office and placed an offer, which was accepted. Nothing could have been simpler. Everything went smoothly with the sale and purchase, and six weeks later, at the beginning of May, we moved in.

A strange atmosphere

As my husband had to work on the day of the move, I obtained the keys myself, and went to pick up my mum, who had agreed to lend a hand. My husband would follow on later with his friend, who was to help with the heavy lifting. I felt so proud as I put the key in the door for the first time. I carried Gemma, who was now five months old, into the hallway, whispering to her how happy she was going to be, in this, her new home, whilst Mum followed closely behind, her arms full of cleaning materials.

As we stood in the hallway, the atmosphere seemed slightly different to the last time I had been in the house. I took Mum into the front room. Without the furniture and curtains, the room looked dingy and unwelcoming. I could tell by her face that she wasn't very impressed. I continued to show her around the house, and we returned to the front room. (In later months, even though it was the least attractive room in the house, this room would become my refuge.)

'Well, what do you think?' I asked.

'You'll not stay here long, our Tracy,' she replied. 'Come on, let's get the kettle on. We've got some serious cleaning to do.' And with that, she promptly turned and left the room and headed for the kitchen.

I ignored her remark, and worked alongside her, scrubbing cupboards, floors, ceilings, and anything else that didn't move! We vacuumed the carpets, cleaned the windows, hung curtains, directed the positioning of furniture, made up the beds, and had a singsong whilst we did it. When all the hard work was finished, I looked around my new home with pride.

That evening, we invited family members round for a tour of inspection. My husband's family arrived first. They had a quick look around, expressed their approval and then left. Later, my brother and brother-in-law dropped in before going out on the town for a few drinks. We left them to take a look around on their own. They had only been upstairs a short time when they both came running back down, laughing their heads off.

'Whatever are you two laughing at?' I asked.

My brother responded by saying, 'Your bathroom's really spooky, Sis.'

'What do you mean?' I queried.

'Well,' he said, 'me and Will just went in there, and it went really cold and icy. We checked the windows to see if there was a draught coming in, but they were all shut tight – then Will thought that someone tapped him on the shoulder.'

William added, 'Yeah, I thought it was Ady messing around, but he was in the shower room, and I was in the bathroom, standing near the sink. There's no way he could have reached me from in there.'

My husband laughed at them, saying, 'You daft devils, you'll have imagined it.'

'Yeah, probably,' Ady replied, but he looked uncomfortable.

Things that go bump...

That night, Gemma was really restless. Whatever methods I tried to settle her down, she just would not sleep. Eventually I brought her into bed with us, and she snuggled up to me peacefully. It won't hurt for tonight, I thought to myself. It must be really strange for her, coming to a new house.

The next day was Saturday and a constant stream of family and friends turned up to view our new home. None of them seemed as keen on it as I was, but at that stage I wasn't bothered about what they thought. In the afternoon, my younger sister Lisa came round with her new boyfriend. I was surprised when she too commented on the 'spooky atmosphere' in the bathroom and at the top of the stairs. However, I paid little attention, assuming that my brother Adrian had put her up to it as some kind of joke. We went to bed early that night, and again Gemma was restless to the point that I felt it necessary to bring her into our own bed.

The first couple of weeks passed in a haze of sorting through boxes, and visitors coming and going. I was exhausted throughout this time because, whatever I tried, Gemma just would not sleep. She screamed and screamed until she felt me close to her. I know that babies will sometimes try it on, but Gemma had never been like this before. I started to become worried – what if she was ill? I took her to the doctor's, where she was given a clean bill of health, and I was advised to be sterner with her, and to ignore her bouts of midnight screaming. This was easier said than done. My husband had recently started a new job with better pay in a local factory, which involved working shifts, and he really needed undisturbed sleep. He was doing two jobs at that time, and I felt guilty that I couldn't seem to get Gemma to settle without fetching her into our bed. I started taking her out in her pram late at night for midnight walks. She would drift off to sleep perfectly well, but as soon as I tried to lift her from her pram to put her into her cot, she would begin to scream. In the end I started sleeping on the settee with her in the pram next to me – but this meant that I was exhausted during the day and felt increasingly unable to cope with my demanding job.

Eventually, my husband and I had a big row one night just before he set off for work. Gemma's sleeping problems had caused a huge rift in our relationship, and I accused him of leaving me to deal with our child alone. I felt he was unsupportive and unrealistic to expect me to shoulder the whole burden. After all, I also had a job. As with any row, nasty and hurtful things were said by both parties, and after my husband left for work I cried myself to sleep, feeling that all my carefully laid plans had gone awry. I awoke at about 1 a.m. to the sound of a strange rattling noise at either side of the bed. My stomach turned over, as I realised that the rattling was the sound of coat hangers in the wardrobes banging against each other. The bed was positioned in the middle of the room with wardrobes in the alcoves on either side. Gemma was in bed with me, and seemed fretful and unsettled as usual. My mind was racing – what was causing the coat hangers to rattle? Had someone got into the bedroom and decided to hide in the wardrobe?

I ran through the darkness to the other side of the room and switched on the light. The rattling continued. I had to find out what was causing it, so I flung open the wardrobe doors. There was nothing and no one there, but to my great surprise, the coat hangers continued to rattle and dance in front of my eyes, the clothes on them swinging limply like strange deformed bodies performing some weird ritualistic dance.

Slamming the wardrobe doors shut, I dived back into bed and hid under the duvet. As a child, when I had been scared of the dark, I curled myself up into a ball in bed, with my knees under my chin, and my head fully covered. Somehow, making myself small in this way made me feel safe from harm. I adopted this position now, with Gemma curled up tightly next to my stomach. As suddenly as it had started, the rattling of coat hangers stopped. After a few minutes I tentatively pulled the duvet back and looked around the room. All seemed peaceful and normal. Gemma was sleeping soundly. I decided to leave the light on and try to get back to sleep. However, my head was spinning, my heart was thumping and my stomach heaving, as I tried to rationalise what I had seen.

Eventually I drifted off to sleep. I was awoken again at about 3 a.m., this time by the bed being shaken violently at the bottom. I looked around the room. What on earth is happening, I thought. Are we having an earthquake? The bed shook violently again; this time one corner lifted completely off the ground. I immediately jumped up, and looked underneath to see what could be causing the bed to move. There was nothing there. The floor was stable, as was the rest of the room; only the bed was shaking, as if someone had taken hold of it and was lifting it up. The room felt heavy and oppressive. I had always felt it to be dark in there, but as I looked around now, the corners of the room seemed dingy and dirty, the atmosphere bleak. I lifted Gemma from the centre of the bed, and quickly left the room.

Downstairs in the sitting room at the front of the house, I switched on the lights, turned on the television, lit the gas fire and settled on the settee. I placed Gemma in her pram and sang to her to get her back to sleep. I tried to work out in my mind what I had just witnessed in my bedroom. Eventually, exhaustion overwhelmed me, and I drifted off to sleep, to be awoken by the return of my husband at about 8 a.m.

'What are you doing in here?' he enquired, as if nothing had happened, as if there had been no row before he went to work. I proceeded to tell him about what I had experienced. He shrugged and laughed. 'You'll have dreamed it all,' he said. 'Either that or it was probably just a load of lorries going past on the road outside.' He seemed unprepared to discuss the subject further and took himself off to bed.

Things get even stranger...

Over the next few weeks, whenever we had visitors, someone always commented about the strange feelings they had at the top of the stairs and in the bathroom area. I also began to feel uncomfortable in the bathroom. One of my great pleasures in life is relaxing in the bath with a good book and music playing in the background. I didn't feel comfortable doing this in our new house because, whenever I went in the bathroom, I felt I was being watched. I even suggested to my husband that the man from next door might have drilled a hole in the wall and been looking through it whenever there was anyone in the bathroom. I became paranoid about going to the toilet during the night, because I felt scared of doing so.

With my husband working shifts, I spent a great deal of time on my own. I always chose to enter the house via the side passage and through the back door. Sometimes, on entering the kitchen, I felt as if my arrival was being acknowledged by the house or some presence within its walls, and in my mind I could hear voices shouting, 'She's here, she's here.' On some occasions when this happened I went straight into the front room where I felt safe from harm, and where the sunshine lit up the four walls, dispelling any thoughts of something or someone hiding in the dark corners. All the time we lived there, I never chose to sit in the other lounge at the back of the house, as I could not bear the dark, overbearing atmosphere in that room. Instead, I would remain in the front room for the best part of the day, only leaving there when it was entirely necessary, to prepare a meal, or fetch a toy for Gemma to play with.

Sometimes the feelings on entering the house were so bad that I would come in through the back door, and go straight down the hallway and leave the house by the front door. On those days I would walk around town for hours with Gemma in her pram. I would visit relatives, and then walk up to the factory where my husband worked and wait for his shift to finish so that I could return home with him.

Because I was tired, I also occasionally had an afternoon nap with Gemma when I got back from work, and we would snuggle up together on my bed. Many times I awoke to the sound of footsteps on the stairs; many times I shouted out my husband's name, thinking he had come home from work early, but there was never anyone there. Whenever I mentioned this to him, he always shrugged it off, saying I had probably heard someone going upstairs in one of the adjoining houses, but I wasn't so sure. The footsteps always seemed so loud, just as if the person was in our house.

One night, at around 9.30 p.m., Gemma was sleeping soundly in her pram in the front room, and I decided to make myself a coffee, and to start preparing my husband's tea as he was due in from work shortly. I switched the light on in the kitchen, turned on the radio, filled the kettle and set it to boil. I sang along to the music as I worked, washing a few pots, cleaning work surfaces, and putting a load of washing into the machine. I stopped a moment to take a sip of coffee, but as I picked up my cup, I felt someone tap me on the shoulder. I spun around so quickly that I spilled my coffee. There was no one there. I looked all around the kitchen, and walked down the hallway to the front room where Gemma lay sleeping. There was no one around. I called out my husband's name, thinking he might have returned home from work early and was playing a trick on me. There was no one in the house except Gemma and myself, so I returned to the kitchen and stood in front of the cooker.

Just then I began to have a strange feeling around my neck and shoulders, as if there was a very light weight pressing down on me. I could feel a presence, as if someone or something was sitting on my back. Tingles went up and down my spine, my legs felt weak and my stomach was heaving.

I was really scared so I turned off the cooker, fetched Gemma in her pram, and went out the front door, deciding to walk up to the factory in the dark to meet my husband. Needless to say, when he saw me and I told him what had happened, he seemed very annoyed. My constant stories of strange things happening in the house were giving him cause for concern, and I felt that he was beginning to doubt my sanity. We went home, and the house felt perfectly normal and welcoming as we entered, and we went to bed as soon as my husband had finished his tea.

I was desperate for something unusual to happen whilst my husband was around so that he too could experience the strange phenomena. Luckily, I didn't have to wait too long. One night about a week later I found myself awake at about 2 a.m. As usual Gemma was cuddled up in bed with us. Suddenly, there was a huge racket from her room next door. My husband leaped out of bed and switched on the light. 'What the hell is that?' he shouted. There was a cacophony of sound coming from the room – bells ringing, music playing, horns sounding, squeaks, bangs, motors running, floorboards creaking. I got out of bed, and we decided to enter Gemma's bedroom together. My husband picked up a hammer from his toolbox in the wardrobe – fully expecting to find an intruder in the room next door. When we switched on the light, the sight that met us was quite unbelievable. Many of Gemma's toys were working on their own: her little music box record-player was merrily playing 'Twinkle Twinkle, Little Star', a lamp she had been given switched itself on and off, some of the baby rattles were rattling, her cot mobile was swinging backwards and forwards, and the train set with a little bell in the engine was tinkling as it rocked from side to side.

But the most frightening sight of all was the child-sized battery-powered car, which was careering around the room, apparently with a mind of its own. The car was red, and my mum and dad had bought it for Gemma for her first Christmas. She had never used it, as she was too small for it at the time. It needed a battery to power it, and there were switches and levers to manipulate to enable it to move around. There was no way it could have accidentally started moving around the room on its own without human assistance. The car drove round and round the room, banging into walls, knocking the cot flying, overturning boxes, before coming to a halt right in front of my husband's feet. 'Now will you believe me?' I screamed. 'This house is haunted!'

All through the night we talked about what we had witnessed. We were at a loss as to what to do, how to deal with what was happening. During this time, my husband confessed that there had been times in the house when he had felt uneasy or uncomfortable, as if someone had been watching or following him – but he said he hadn't wanted to frighten me by mentioning it. Oh, how I wished he had told me this earlier! Then we might have been able to do something about it sooner.

Getting help

The next day, I decided the obvious person to speak to was my mum. After all, she was into all that weird Spiritualism stuff, wasn't she? Surely she would be able to get someone to come and exorcise the place for us. I called round to see her that morning and told her what had been happening. She didn't seem at all surprised, and also confessed that she had sometimes felt uneasy in the house. She agreed to help me by coming round with a friend of hers named Gwynneth, who was also a medium. Together they would 'tune in' to the vibrations, to see if they could make contact with whoever or whatever was causing the problem.

Mum agreed that she and Gwyn would call round the following night at 7 p.m. I spent the day nervously anticipating their arrival. I cleaned the house from top to bottom, arranged flowers in the lounge, placed pot pourri in the bathroom, swept the doorstep, and made it look as welcoming as possible. Keeping myself busy somehow kept me from thinking about the possibility that the house I was living in was haunted.

My husband came home from work and we had our tea together. Gemma was playing happily in front of the fire, and I had just switched on the TV, when there was a knock at the front door. It was Mum and Gwyn. I ushered them in and offered them a coffee. 'No, not just yet, Trace,' Gwyn said. 'We'll have one later on, luvvie, when we've had a look around.'

Gwynneth, like my mum, is a small lady in height, but quite large in build. Her hair is also a similar style to Mum's, but lighter in colour – they are often mistaken for sisters. I briefly explained to Gwyn about the strange things I had been experiencing in the house. She made no comment, but asked me to show her and Mum around. They had already seen the lounge, so we moved into the other sitting room. Then we went into the kitchen, and after that, moved upstairs. In the bathroom, Gwyn stood quite still and the expression on her face changed – she looked slightly concerned. Eventually, she directed me to continue the tour. We stayed briefly in the back bedroom, then stood a while in the front bedroom; again, Gwyn's expression was thoughtful. After standing awhile on the landing at the top of the stairs, we glanced inside the small front bedroom, then made our way downstairs.

I couldn't wait to hear the verdict. We returned to the lounge at the front of the house and sat down. The room was in darkness, lit only by the light of a small table lamp, the fire and the TV screen, so there was a kind of spooky atmosphere as we all took our places. I was desperate to know what could be done to stop all the strange happenings, and so I perched on the edge of the settee opposite Gwyn, and looked at her expectantly.

She herself was looking intently at the wall behind me. I couldn't help but glance over my shoulder, and although there was nothing there, I began to feel scared!

'Well now,' she said. 'It is time. . .'

'Time for what?' I enquired, tentatively.

'Time for you to begin your work,' she replied.

'What work?' I asked, feeling confused and irritable. She was talking in riddles.

'Your work as a medium, of course!' she said.

I couldn't believe what I was hearing. This couldn't be right – was she going mad? I had no intention of working as a medium, so why was Gwyn saying all this? And what was she looking at behind me? As if she had read my mind, she answered my query.

'I can see a face on the wall behind you; it is your spirit guide. He is a very powerful man indeed. He will make you work hard, and he will not tolerate imperfections. I am glad he isn't my own guide,' she laughed. Then she added, 'He has come to help you, for you have unwittingly unleashed a whole truckload of psychic energy in this house, and a variety of spirits are feeding on it and causing some difficulties for you.'

I looked at her in total bewilderment, as I hadn't a clue what she was talking about. This must have shown on my face, for suddenly she raised her voice and snapped, 'There's nothing wrong with the house, you silly girl – it's you!'

We sat talking for ages afterwards, drinking coffee and eating biscuits. Gwynneth explained to me that I had an innate ability to work with the spirit people, and somehow I was unleashing energy into the atmosphere, which attracted them to me, and into the house. Looking back now, I find it quite uncanny that the name Gwynneth was linked to my being told that I was a medium, just as it was to Paul being told the same thing.

Before she left, Gwynneth advised me that I must learn to control the energy levels, thereby controlling the spirit contacts. She said it would be wise to attend the Spiritualist church to receive proper training. In the meantime, I was to send thoughts out to the spirits, telling them that I was not yet ready to work with them. She said I should ask them to stop scaring me, and to stop using my energy in the way that they had been.

Meeting my guide

Surely this couldn't be happening? I was just a normal 22-year-old woman with a husband and baby. I didn't want to be a medium, I didn't want to talk to dead people. None of this fitted in with the life I had mapped out for myself.

That night I went to bed feeling very confused. Maybe I would go to the Spiritualist church, maybe I wouldn't. For the first time in ages, I slept peacefully, and so did Gemma. When I woke the next day, I decided I was having none of this. I didn't want to be a medium, and I was *not* going to pass on messages from dead people. However, I began practising the techniques Gwynneth had described to me the night before – talking away in my mind, asking for help to control what was happening, politely requesting that the spirit people stop frightening me, and that I be left alone to lead my life in peace.

This obviously did not work, for that afternoon, as Gemma was having her nap and I was lounging on the settee with a book, I began to feel drowsy, and I too nodded off into a half-sleeping state. I was awoken by the feeling of a presence in the room. I felt as though I was being watched by a large man, but could not as yet distinguish what he looked like. I heard a booming voice, which commanded me to pay attention, and listen to his words. I could hear music, the sound of drums, and the feeling of the presence grew into a vision of a Native American Indian standing before me in full headdress. He was quite stunning to look at. Could this be the gentleman Gwynneth had spoken of, the night before? I felt scared, but at peace. I was bewildered, but also filled with wonder at what I was seeing.

The Indian spoke again. 'Child, you cannot forsake your destiny,' he said. 'There is no point asking us to leave, for we cannot go. We have been sent to guide you along the pathway you are meant to travel, a road which will be long and arduous, but vibrant and fulfilling.' With this he was gone.

I rubbed my eyes, wondering what had happened. Had I just seen a Native American Indian in my front room? I was convinced I was going mad.

So much had happened in so short a time, I was finding it difficult to take it all in. One thing I knew for certain, though: I was now feeling totally out of my depth. I decided that I needed help – and fast. . .

CHAPTER 6
Paul: Divine intervention

I was soon visiting College Road Spiritualist church again on a regular basis and my mediumship was benefiting greatly from the practice I gained whilst working in the open circle.

On my first visit dear Edie had been very pleased to see me.

'Hello, stranger,' she said, with a glint in her eye.

'We thought you'd passed on,' she added, chuckling at her reference to the fact that I hadn't been to church for a while whilst attending Sandy's teaching group.

'Afraid not, Edie, you've got me for a long time yet,' I replied. I was surprised to see how many people had turned up for the circle. There must have been over 80 of them crammed into the room. I took my seat and watched quietly as everyone else took theirs. I noticed one lady who was obviously very grief-stricken, and before the circle started I sent a special thought out to the spirit world, asking that they come and help her.

A short while later, I got up and walked over to where this lady was seated. 'I have a young lady here who tells me her name is Angela,' I said. 'She's telling me that she passed with cancer and that you helped to look after her before she passed.

Are you Janet?' The lady nodded. I could see that she was crying.

'Angela wants me to thank you for all the help and love you gave to her,' I went on gently. 'She says you really did put yourself out.'

'That's true,' came Janet's reply, whilst dabbing her eyes.

'She must only be about 29,' I said, 'and she's singing "happy birthday",' I continued.

'That's right, she passed on her twenty-ninth birthday,' Janet confirmed.

That was all I had to say to Janet, so I gave her Angela's love and sat down. When the circle had finished, Janet thanked me.

Edie had been listening in and, as always, offered some advice.

'You must remember that it's the spirit world who need thanking, Paul, for what are you without them?' I agreed and quickly said a silent 'Thank you'. Edie was very good at helping me keep my feet on the ground whilst developing my understanding of my gift.

A new path opens up

The time to start taking services on my own soon arrived. I can remember being out of the house nearly every night of the week visiting one Spiritualist church or another, come wind, rain or sunshine. Because I hadn't yet taken my driving test, I relied on friends to give me lifts so I could honour my bookings.

I was also studying hard and tried to fit my coursework in late at night after I came back from church, or during my lunchtimes. At that time, I mainly took services in Yorkshire, and continued to go to the 'open circle' at College Road. However, as my reputation grew, I began to receive offers of work from further afield.

One evening, I was sitting quietly in church, when a lady tapped me on the shoulder.

'Paul Norton?' she asked. I nodded in response, wondering who she was.

'I have seen you work and I think you are a really good medium.'

She continued, 'I was wondering if you would consider taking a charity meeting for the hospice appeal? I know of a room we can use, and I'm sure that a lot of people would support us.'

I agreed to help and, without further ado, she wrote down a couple of dates for me to check and gave me her telephone number.

I telephoned a couple of days later and everything was agreed: I was to take my first public meeting outside a Spiritualist church!

Little did I know it, but the spirit people were opening up a new pathway for me.

Over the following weeks, I noticed that there seemed to be a kind of 'buzz' in the air. People at church would whisper and point at me. Neighbours who lived in the same street were giving me strange looks. I couldn't fathom what was going on, and was starting to feel a bit paranoid! Then, one day when I was in town, a poster in a shop window caught my eye. In large bold letters it said:

'A CHARITY EVENING OF CLAIRVOYANCE
IN AID OF THE HOSPICE APPEAL
IS TO BE HELD AT THE FAIRWAY HOTEL
WITH MEDIUM PAUL NORTON.'

Now I realised why there were so many strange looks, whispers and people pointing whenever I was out and about. It didn't end there, though. The following day I received a message from the lady organising the event. Apparently the local paper wanted to do a feature on me in order to create more interest in the appeal.

The newspaper arranged for a reporter to visit me, and to take down some details. I answered the questions and chatted about various other topics. When the article came out, I was even more embarrassed than I had been when I first saw the posters, as the headline read: 'POWERFUL PAUL!' The article went on to say how I'd been gifted with special powers of clairvoyancy.

I'd never even mentioned the word powers and I certainly didn't consider myself to be gifted. As for the use of the word 'clairvoyancy' – the article made it sound as if I was some kind of Blackpool Pier fortune-teller. However, it must have done some good as the tickets soon sold out.

The evening came round all too quickly, and suddenly I felt very nervous indeed. I arrived at the hotel early so I could get changed and have a little rest in the small room they'd set aside for me. I tried to focus my mind on making a link with Naiomi, asking for her help, and the support of anyone else in the spirit world that could join me, to help make this evening a success.

I paced the corridors, trying everything I could think of to calm myself down and to stop my nerves from getting the better of me. Eventually it was time to start!

I walked through to the main hall, and entered just as my name was being announced to the capacity audience.

As I walked up onto the stage, my heart flipped. However, I soon managed to compose myself and started the evening by explaining how mediumship worked, and what would be happening.

Then I started delivering messages.

One young girl who had passed to the spirit world with leukaemia made an emotional return to speak to her mother and older sister, who were present in the audience. She was able to tell us about the colour and style of the clothes her mother had dressed her in for her burial. Apparently, they had been her favourite ones.

She ended the message by telling the audience, 'I've got my golden locks back now.' And her mother was overcome by tears of joy at this news.

A father in the spirit world was reunited with two of his five daughters in the audience. Amidst the tears, he was able to joke with the ladies that one of them had dyed her hair that afternoon. 'She should have been blonde, not orange,' he quipped, adding, 'she didn't leave it on long enough – she should have read the instructions better. She's always in too much of a hurry, that one.'

This caused everyone, including the lady concerned, to fall into fits of giggles.

Message after message was delivered, and the room was filled with every conceivable emotion as the spirit people worked hard to make their presence felt. The evening flew by. None of us wanted it to end. It was a tremendous success for the charity, the spirit world and the audience. A lot of the people present stayed behind to ask questions and many wanted to book private sittings.

I explained that my college work was my priority at that moment, but people still insisted that they be allowed to book in advance.

Meeting Pam

One of the messages I gave out that night was for a lady called Pam and her daughter Sally Ann. Afterwards she wrote to me ...

Dear Paul,

My daughter and I attended your meeting at the Fairway Hotel a few months ago. You picked my daughter out for a message – she was the girl sitting right towards the back of the hall.

You said that there was a man in the spirit world communicating, who'd been in the Army and spent a lot of time in India and also France. This was her grandfather. He told you that my daughter, who you first went to, was pregnant, which she was and he was showing you pink booties. My daughter has since had a little girl.

You spoke of the problems around her, of which there were a lot, and you said it would all work out. It has done. You said he was with Mary – well, Mary is his first wife. You said that the lady sitting next to my daughter was her mother, which was true: it was me. You then moved over to me and told me about the new business

87

venture which I was starting and said that it would really take off.
I had just opened a shop and it has taken off. You mentioned my
daughter's baby again and said that she would be just like her in
looks – in fact, she's her double.

You said the man had passed away with emphysema, which had
started when he was in the war. In fact, he'd spent two days in the
sea at Dunkirk and this eventually caused him problems later on.
This was all correct. You then said that he was Irish and that he
had ginger hair, again correct. I just wanted to thank you for the
help you gave to us that evening.

Pam,

Doncaster

Pam and I kept in touch, and I later learned she was a Tarot
card reader with her own business in the town. We decided
it would be fun to give each other a reading each New Year.
During one particular reading Pam mentioned three specific
things, all of which eventually came true, although not within
the timescales I would have expected.

She told me I would shortly be coming into contact with a
young lady with dark hair, who I had known for many years
and who would seek me out for help in coming to terms with
the loss of a loved one.

She then told me that I would help another friend in need,
who had lost her husband, the husband being somewhere
between 45 and 55 years old.

Finally, she told me that I would one day meet a lady
medium the same age as myself, who would become a very
strong influence upon me and my work and my life.

Some time later I received a telephone call from a young lady who wished to book a sitting. Such was my reputation, and her strong determination to see me, that she and her mum had gone to my mother's house to obtain my telephone number in order to make contact with me. Needless to say, my mum wasn't too pleased to have people knocking on her door like this.

I booked an appointment for her to come and see me, and when she arrived, I realised that I knew her. In fact, I'd known her since I was about 12, as she lived at the top of the street where I grew up.

It turned out that she had recently lost her boyfriend in a freak accident and she was looking for some answers to her many questions and some sort of contact from him, if possible. Fortunately I was able to help her, and her boyfriend communicated a lovely message to her, which gave her tremendous strength. I was really pleased when I received this letter a few days later:

Dear Paul,

After my boyfriend passed away on 6th April this year, I had feelings I have never felt before. As if someone in my head was angry and wanted to tell me something. It felt like someone was shaking me saying, 'It's me, I need to talk to you.'

In order to find out what was happening, I sought out your telephone number and booked a sitting.

Although I have known you for years, having gone to the same school, I have not seen or spoken to you since 1982. You couldn't possibly have known what had happened to me in between time. Also, we moved quite a few years ago, from the estate where you used to live.

The details you gave me about my boyfriend, his family, friends and his accident, have proved to me, beyond any shadow of a doubt, that someone must have told you whilst I was there in your house. That someone being my boyfriend and the spirit world.

It has helped me very much to know that he is not dead and gone, and that he'll be there to greet me when I eventually pass over.

Thank you,

Joanne

Pam had been right with her reading. I had known this person for years, and I had not seen or spoken to her since 1982. She did have dark hair, just as Pam had said, and she was in need of a great deal of help.

The prediction about the other lady coming to me for help after losing her husband was a bit too close for comfort. It was actually Pam herself whose husband passed away later that same year.

He was 56, just over the age which Pam had mentioned in her reading.

It was quite difficult for me to help her get over this sad loss because I had such a close connection to her, but I hope I was able to offer her some comfort and make things a bit easier. She did continue working hard afterwards, booking in lots of readings and hypnotherapy sessions. We also joined forces to start a small development group, which was well attended.

The spirit world provides

Two of Pam's predictions had been so uncannily accurate, that, for the whole of that year, I expected to meet up with a female medium who would somehow help me with my own work. Sadly, this never happened, and eventually I pushed the thought to the back of my mind, and continued to work alone until such time as the spirit people saw fit to change things.

After the Fairway Hotel event, a number of other organisations approached me for similar bookings and work started to snowball.

My studies, however, were beginning to suffer and so I made the difficult decision to cut down on the meetings. I also decided to get a part-time job to see me through college. I'd had to give up my job at the nightclub when I started the course, and the grant that I'd received had nearly run out. Because most of the meetings I was taking at the time were for charity, I rarely received any payment for doing them. I asked the spirit world for some help, as I still had to support myself financially in order to be able to do their work. Much to my surprise, Naiomi immediately advised me to go to my local Job Centre, where I would find the ideal part-time job.

I did as she said, and, as I scanned the vacancy boards the next day, one advert caught my eye. It was for a Senior Night Care Officer in a residential home for elderly people. The job was at a place called Wyndthorpe Hall, and I was offered an immediate interview. I agreed to go, even though I felt I was dressed inappropriately at the time.

When I arrived I was asked to complete an application form. The lady in the office took the form from me and told me that they would be in touch. I was disappointed by the way I'd been treated and felt I'd wasted my time. On the bus home, Naiomi whispered in my ear.

'Be patient, just wait ten days.'

I did as I was told, but still applied for other jobs.

Exactly ten days after I had applied, I received confirmation that I had been successful.

Naiomi had been right yet again.

Wyndthorpe Hall was a very large stately home, which had been refurbished to make it suitable for elderly people. The foyer was massive, with thick-pile velvety carpets. Suspended some 40 feet in the air was a huge brass chandelier. It must have been at least four feet wide. Above it was a very large glass dome, which housed the brass chain mountings that held the chandelier in place.

The rest of the Hall was a mixture of old and new, but it had been tastefully decorated to make the residents feel as comfortable as possible. I was to work regularly on nights with Christine, a trained nurse. We hit it off straight away, and I instantly knew I was going to enjoy working there.

Spirits to the rescue

Time passed quickly, and Chris and I became very good workmates. After cleaning the rooms and helping the residents to bed, we would often sit together in the foyer, have our supper and chat. Chris knew that I was a medium, because some of her friends had seen me work. One night, she told me that Wyndthorpe had a resident ghost and asked if I could 'tune in' and find out more about the spirit in question.

I hated being put on the spot like this, but I just said, 'If they decide to come and talk to me, I'll see what I can find out.' After that I completely forgot about the conversation and concentrated on my work.

A few nights later, at around 2.30 a.m., Chris had just asked me if I wanted a drink.

'Tea please, Chris,' I shouted, as she walked off into the kitchen. I took up my usual seat in the foyer, right under the chandelier. I was very tired, but I could hear Chris in the distance, washing the cups in the sink, and busying herself with making the tea. Suddenly, I heard an almighty bang, which sent me running up the stairs towards where the noise had come from. At the same time, my pager started bleeping and showed a call coming from bedroom number three. I rushed down the corridor, and entered the room in question.

As I walked through the door, I realised that bedroom three was empty. I stood in the doorway for a moment gathering my thoughts, and noticed that the emergency button for this room was under the bed.

Chris shouted up, 'Everything all right, Paul?'

Before I had a chance to answer, my pager started bleeping again. The alert was again for bedroom three. I couldn't understand what was happening as I was actually standing in that room and there was no one else there, yet the button had been pushed to call for assistance. Something very strange was going on.

Chris came rushing up the stairs, to find out what was wrong. I looked at her in a state of shock and hurriedly explained what had happened.

'I guess it must be the ghost you mentioned, Chris,' I said. Just to be on the safe side, we decided to check on each resident. We also double checked all the doors and windows and had a quick look around the outside of the building. There were no signs of anything unusual. In fact, it seemed to be a fairly quiet, still night.

About 20 minutes later, Chris was half-heartedly browsing through a magazine, when I asked her if she could feel a cold breeze. She nodded and said that she was a bit chilly; we looked around to see where the draught might be coming from.

'It seems to be coming down from the ceiling,' I said, looking up as I did so. What happened next was really spooky! To our utter disbelief, the huge chandelier above us began swinging from side to side.

I was starting to feel a little shaky by this time, and decided to send a thought out to my spirit friend Naiomi.

Within a matter of seconds, I felt her calming influence. She told me in a matter-of-fact manner that the spirit who was causing the disturbance was that of a lady who'd been murdered in that very spot some 200 years ago. Naiomi said that this lady had on many occasions tried to make her presence felt. Well, she's certainly succeeding tonight, I thought! Naiomi went on to say that the lady had been a maid to the Lord of the Manor. It had been one of her particular duties to polish the chandelier and all the brasses.

I relayed the information to Chris, who was sitting beside me, and she confirmed that there had been a story about one of the maids being murdered by a stable-hand.

Chris went on to tell me that, strangely enough, when the Hall was being renovated there was a report about some human bones being found under the floorboards where the cellar had been. We were both intrigued by what had happened, and by the information Naiomi had given me. However, Naiomi hadn't finished. She went on to say, 'There is a problem with the lift. It must be mended to avoid danger. The maid has come to warn you of this. She doesn't wish any of you any harm.'

I told Chris about the lift, and we decided to tell the day staff in the morning.

They were also aware that I was a medium, so when Chris told them about the lift they said they would get the engineer to take a look at it. On returning to work that evening, Sheila, one of the day care assistants, told me that the lift had collapsed just after Chris and I had left. She said there had been four people in it, and it had taken the Fire Brigade two hours to get them out. Apparently, the Chief Fire Officer said he couldn't believe that no one had been injured as the lift had been literally hanging on by a thread. Sheila patted me on the back before she went on her way, and shouted, 'Keep up the good work, Paul!'

This wasn't the first time that the spirit world had warned me of impending danger. Through my work in the local churches, I was introduced to a lady called Lynn, who had apparently been experiencing weird occurrences in her house. For instance, she was sure that she'd heard a baby crying on several occasions, even though she had been alone in the house.

As Lynn was starting to feel quite desperate, I agreed to take a look. I don't know quite what I was expecting, but, when I arrived at her home, I found a fairly modern, un-assuming, neatly-kept, semi-detached house. I walked around outside for a few minutes to get a feel of the place before going in. When I entered the property, I was guided upstairs to a spare room right at the front of the house. I could distinctly hear the sound of a baby – not crying, as I had been expecting, but gurgling away happily. As I looked at the spare bed there, I visualised the outline of a small child and immediately noticed something white around its neck. I was also very aware of a smell of gas within the room. I decided I should ask Naiomi for help.

She told me that the previous occupant of the house had lost a small baby, who had got caught up in his bedclothes and choked. This would possibly explain why Lynn thought she had heard a baby crying. Naiomi also told me that the gas heater on the landing was leaking badly, and that I was to tell Lynn to get it checked out as soon as possible.

I relayed all this information to Lynn and she phoned the Gas Board immediately. Within 15 minutes an engineer arrived, examined the heater in question and announced that it was very badly fractured. In fact, his words were: 'This is a death trap! I'll have to cut off your gas supply, and take it straight out.'

Although I felt I had done a good job, and once again prevented a harmful situation, I couldn't help feeling sad about the little baby who had died in the house. I decided that, before I left, I would send a thought out to the spirit world to help the baby and bring peace to the house. Almost immediately I became aware of an elderly lady. She appeared to be cuddling the baby and smiling peacefully. I gave a sigh of relief, and felt that my job was done.

A few days later, a very grateful Lynn got in touch to tell me that everything I had said about the previous owner losing a baby had been confirmed by a neighbour. Nobody had wanted to live in the house afterwards because of this.

In these two cases, the people in the spirit world helped by warning of danger. My experience is that they often work behind the scenes, engineering situations and lending a helping hand.

The spirit people not only help us avoid the not-so-nice things, they also advise on the positive situations in our lives, assisting us wherever possible. Our loved ones look after us when they are alive, so it is only natural that they should want to watch over and help us from the other side.

Over the years, I have found their help and guidance invaluable. I have also had the sense that certain parts of my life have been arranged so that I could continue my important work as a medium. This may seem a strange statement to make. However, on many occasions during my life, I have felt as if it wasn't me making the choices about my future, but some far greater force that had plans for me, of which I was not always aware.

When I enrolled at college, I hadn't expected to be working as a medium at the same time. Getting my college work done, as well as demonstrating mediumship was a very difficult balancing act, and it wasn't easy to manage financially.

As I was nearing the end of my course, I began to wonder how I would be able to hold down a fulltime job and continue to work as a medium. I had come to love my spiritual work and didn't want to give it up. However, I couldn't see how I could put enough effort into my mediumship to continue to progress, whilst at the same time earning enough to be financially stable. It seemed that I was in need of some divine intervention.

Finding the right place

During the last term of college, I was asked to do a placement in a residential home for people with physical disabilities. During this placement my life for the next 16 years was to be mapped out quite unexpectedly, and my worries over how I would continue with mediumship and find a way to support myself were laid to rest.

Whilst I was there I met a young disabled lad by the name of Daz, who was around the same age as myself. We became good friends, having the same sense of humour and outlook on life. Daz hated the home, and wanted to escape the situation he was in. He looked to me for assistance, and asked if I would consider looking after him within the community if he could find somewhere to live. At the time his suggestion seemed an ideal solution to my problem. Looking after Daz would give me a certain amount of freedom to do my spiritual work, whilst also offering a regular income, and a better lifestyle for him. Everyone would benefit. Now all we had to do was sort out somewhere to live.

We went to the local council offices, but discovered that there was an eight-year wait for suitable accommodation, so we made the decision to rent privately.

I was very aware of Naiomi's presence around this time and she guided us to look at a flat that had just become available. Although it needed decorating, we decided to take it.

We moved in two weeks later and friends helped out in a number of ways, bringing presents and bits of furniture. For the next 16 years, Daz was to be my constant companion. He accompanied me to church services and theatres to watch me work, and had the pleasure of meeting many of the country's best mediums, including Gordon Higginson, who always had a kind word and a smile for him.

Of course, I couldn't do it all on my own, and I relied heavily on other people over the coming months and years to help care for Daz on occasions when I was unable to take him with me. Joanne, the young woman who had lost her boyfriend, introduced me to her mother Maureen, and I paid them both to do care work on a regular basis. Through my work as a medium, I became friendly with Gail and Paul Buckley, who also joined the payroll and helped care for Daz over the coming years.

Daz became more and more independent, and learnt new skills, which later enabled him to make the decision to return to a more conventional caring environment. In return, he helped me to be humble and to be grateful for my physical strengths, and looking after him also gave me the freedom to work as a medium.

One of the best housewarming presents Daz and I received was from Pauline, who used to give me lifts to Sandy's development circle. She now lived just around the corner from us, and would be a welcome visitor over the coming weeks.

One afternoon she called in on us, carrying a small box under her arm.

'I've brought you both a present,' she said, with a cheeky smile. She opened the box and a small black, white and tan puppy popped its head out. She was a Jack Russell Terrier, and I decided to call her Gyp. She was a real character, and brought so much fun and laughter into our lives.

One time, a few days before Christmas, I had bought some little chocolate snowmen and Santas to hang on the tree. As I finished decorating it, I stood back to admire my handiwork. At that moment the telephone rang, and I started to have a chat with a friend, who I hadn't heard from for some time.

Imagine my horror when, halfway through the call, I noticed that the Christmas tree was rocking from side to side, the baubles and lights swinging ominously. My heart leapt in my chest. Could it be the spirits making the Christmas tree move in such a strange way? I felt slightly scared as I looked towards the jingling, jangling object, which seemed to have taken on a life of its own. I made an excuse to cut my telephone call short and stared in amazement at the tree.

All of a sudden, gravity took hold and the tree toppled over-Accompanied by a loud yelp, Gyp ran out, looking somewhat surprised and upset that her impromptu feast of chocolate snowmen had come to such an abrupt and unsatisfactory end!

Life was good. I had a secure job and comfortable home, and so I felt I no longer needed to continue my college studies. Daz and I were doing all the things that 20-year-olds enjoy doing and both of us were benefiting from the situation.

Daz was happy to be living independently in the local community and he was as intrigued by the spirit world as I was. Finally, all my problems appeared to be resolving themselves, and my mediumship was able to progress further as the spirit world created many new openings and experiences for me over the coming years.

CHAPTER 7
Tracy: Testing the water

After Mum and Gwyn had been to visit my house to see if it was haunted, the problems hadn't ceased. In fact, things had got decidedly worse. I had come to the end of my tether, and I really needed help to sort things out. I decided to follow Gwynneth's advice and visit Mum's Spiritualist church.

I was very nervous about my first visit, as I had no idea what to expect. When I arrived, a number of people were already seated around the room, and I noticed Gwynneth sitting in the front row, chattering to the women on either side of her. She saw me come in and nodded, as if indicating that she agreed with my decision to attend the meeting. Mum directed me to a seat at the back. I was handed a hymn book, told to sit down and informed that the service would start shortly. I sat in the corner and was filled with fear. I didn't have a clue about what would happen and at that point I could easily have got up and walked out.

Suddenly everyone went quiet, as the medium approached the table at the top of the room and sat in the chair on the left-hand side. My mum stood, and addressed the congregation.

'Good evening, ladies and gentlemen,' she announced. 'I would like to give you all a very warm welcome to Retford

Spiritualist Society.' She paused whilst everyone responded with their own 'good evenings'. Then she gave the number of the first hymn and everyone began to sing.

After the hymn-singing the medium said a prayer and explained his philosophy.

I was intrigued and enthralled by his words. I hadn't realised that Spiritualism was actually a whole philosophy, a way of life, a way of being. I remember thinking that this was a bit like being in church on a Sunday morning and listening to a sermon from a vicar.

The medium then began to point people out and tell them about their 'dead' relatives. He described how people had looked, what types of jobs they had done, and the illnesses they had suffered during their lives. He gave out names, and relevant dates of anniversaries such as birthdays or deaths. He delivered about six messages and then sat down. Another hymn was sung, a closing prayer said, and the service was over.

Eventually Mum approached me and invited me to stay for the 'open circle'. She went on to explain: 'After the service has ended we usually have a drink and something to eat, and then we all sit round in a circle, and try to see if any of us can receive messages to pass on to other members of the group. It gives us all a chance to practise and for new mediums to develop their gifts.'

This all sounded a bit scary, but I was really interested to hear more messages so I agreed to stay.

Whilst the drinks were being served, the chairs were rearranged to form a large circle and the main lights were switched off. The strip light in the kitchen area remained on, and threw a small amount of light into the centre of the room. The circle was about to begin and Gwynneth advised us to find a seat. I chose a seat next to Mum, as I was feeling more than a little apprehensive.

Gwynneth told everyone to link hands, and then began to speak in a very deep and commanding voice.

'I want you all to imagine that the middle of this circle is filled with colour and light,' she began. 'Hold the colours and the light in your mind, and when you are ready, use your mind to imagine that you are passing the light to the person on the left of you.' After a pause, she continued, 'Then, when you are ready, pass the light to the person on the right of you.' She didn't say anything for quite some time, and the members of the circle sat silently. The room was in near-darkness and there was an air of expectancy and anticipation as Gwynneth finally announced, 'This circle is now open.'

I was slightly bemused by all this rigmarole. I didn't fully understand what was going on, and I had had my eyes open all the time that Gwynneth was 'opening up' the circle. I had glanced round at everyone's faces and noticed that they all looked very serious, their eyes squeezed tightly shut, their hands joined lightly together.

No one said anything for what seemed like ages – they merely sat with their eyes closed. Then, suddenly, after about five minutes, a lady sitting opposite me gave a message to the elderly lady named Edna, who had been sitting by the door selling raffle tickets. She was given some fairly basic informa-tion about suffering from a bad back and taking lots of pain-killers. The woman who had given the message to Edna sat down and closed her eyes again.

The evening continued in this vein, with different members

of the circle taking it in turns to stand up and give messages to each other. I was impressed to see that my mum gave several messages to other people in the group.

After about an hour it was time for the circle to end. Gwynneth went around everyone in the group asking them individually if they had any further messages to give before the circle was shut down. When she stopped at me I immediately answered no. I was sure I hadn't received any messages to pass on. I had been far too interested in watching and listening to everyone else to try and tune into the spirits myself.

Mum, however, had different ideas. She intercepted by asking,

'Have you got any words in your mind, or maybe pictures or colours?' I said no. She persisted, 'Well then, is there anyone in the room you are drawn to in particular?'

Without really thinking, I pointed to a pretty girl sitting almost opposite myself within the group.

'Why do you feel drawn to this young woman?' asked Mum.

I answered that I felt the young girl looked sad, and was troubled about something. 'What else?' she asked.

I went on to say that I had the name of Julie in my mind, and that for some strange reason I could see a pair of ice skates. I went on to say that I could also see an image of a young man in my mind. I finished by saying that the young man kept pointing to his throat.

The girl burst into tears. She confirmed that her own name was Julie, that she had gone ice skating on her birthday, and when she returned home she had found her boyfriend dead. Unfortunately he had taken his own life by hanging himself.

'Go on, carry on,' pushed my mum. Everyone else in the circle looked on with interest. I closed my eyes to concentrate, when suddenly all hell broke loose.

I opened my eyes to see that my mum was clutching her throat and she began shouting, 'I can't breathe, I'm choking, Gwyn, please, you've got to help me.'

I was really scared, I didn't know what was happening; I could see that my mum was really distressed.

She left her seat and staggered to the other side of the room, where Gwyn was sitting. By this time, she was retching. Gwyn guided her to a seat and placed both hands on her shoulders. She began speaking in a very hushed voice, using soothing tones to calm Mum down.

Just as I began to feel that a degree of normality had been restored, another of the circle members moved from her seat, also clutching her throat and retching. 'Help me,' she squealed. 'Help me! I'm choking.'

I froze in my seat dismayed by what was happening. I wanted to step in and help sort out this difficult situation but didn't know how to.

Gwynneth urged everyone to remain in their seats to keep the circle closed. She explained that it was important to keep the energy within the circle and not to create any openings whereby energy from outside could come in.

I began to recite the Lord's Prayer in my mind. I was scared that I might be the next person to be overcome by the feelings of choking and nausea.

I like to think that my prayers helped, for, shortly after I had started praying, the pandemonium within the circle ended just as quickly as it had begun. Everyone who had been suffering from the strange symptoms of choking and nausea slumped in their seats.

Gwynneth quickly brought the proceedings to a close. She made everyone link hands and said a brief prayer. Afterwards, she explained that the young man who had hanged himself had tried to get a message through to his girlfriend. Apparently, because of the way he had died, it had been difficult for him to communicate without some of the sitters in the circle feeling what he himself had felt just before he had passed away.

I couldn't believe what I had witnessed. I was very unhappy about the whole situation, and after checking that my mum was OK, I left the meeting and returned home.

Night-time fears

That night, I didn't sleep very well. I still felt uneasy about the apparently uncontrollable spirit who had taken over the circle and I couldn't believe how such a pleasant experience had suddenly turned so sour. I spent most of that night thinking about all the things that had happened since we had come to live in the house at Moorgate. I remembered all the scary feelings I had experienced whilst we had lived here, the strange noises, inanimate objects moving of their own volition, and how finally all of this had brought me through the doors of a Spiritualist church. So far, my experiences with Spiritualism and the spirit world had all been rather unpleasant.

The next morning, Mum phoned at around 8.30 a.m. She seemed hesitant and on edge as she asked me how I was feeling. I told her I hadn't slept very well. She responded by telling me that what had happened during the open circle was extremely unusual, and that it was the first time she had witnessed anything like that in all the years she had spent visiting other Spiritualist churches, as well as running her own.

She then continued by saying how impressed she had been by the message I had given during the circle, and that she thought I had the makings of a decent medium. She offered a great deal of encouragement, and told me that I had a wonderful gift, which I should try to develop. She invited me to the church again next Saturday, but I said I wasn't really sure if I wanted to come along as I felt very put off by the whole experience. We ended by having a bit of a chat about other family members; she asked how Gemma was, and then she had to go.

I spent the rest of that day trying to do 'normal' things like playing with Gemma, doing a bit of housework, and then settling down with the Sunday newspapers. I felt fairly relaxed and comfortable, having pushed the scary events of the night before to the back of my mind.

When my husband came home from work later that day, I told him about what I had experienced the night before, and surprisingly he seemed quite interested – especially when I told him my mum thought I had special powers and that I could give messages from 'dead people'. He said he thought I should go back to the church again next week, and he even offered to come with me!

That night, I couldn't get to sleep. My mind was still full of the recent events and the conversations I had had with Mum and my husband. They had both been really keen for me to continue going to the church and to begin working as a medium, but I was not so sure that this was what I wanted to do. I couldn't see how allowing Spiritualism to become part of my life could possibly work. I had a very demanding job, and had just applied for promotion to the next grade of executive officer. If I was successful with my application, I would have to travel to Mansfield every day – 20 miles away from Retford – and it was a full-time position, whereas I currently only worked part-time.

I was also unsure about whether I would be confident enough to stand up in front of people. At 22 years old I wasn't a particularly confident or outgoing person, and I was extremely shy in new company. Speaking in front of an audience was the last thing I ever imagined myself doing.

Eventually, I fell asleep, my mind a muddle of thoughts and questions about my present situation, and what the future might hold. At around 3 a.m. I awoke very suddenly, with a strange feeling of being watched. I immediately thought that the house was up to its old tricks again – after all, wasn't it the house that had got me into this Spiritualism lark in the first place? I cautiously glanced around the room. It was very dark, the only available light coming from the luminous face of the alarm clock on the table at the other side of the bed where my husband slept.

As my eyes became more focused, I thought I could see something floating above us. I peered into the blackness, and was shocked and frightened to see the figure of an elderly gentleman floating face down about three or four feet in the air, immediately above the bed.

I promptly put my head under the duvet. My breath was coming in short sharp bursts, and my heart was pounding so fast that my chest ached. I nudged my husband, urging him to wake up because I was scared. He grunted and turned over .'What do you want?' asked.

'I'm really scared,' I replied, 'There's someone here in the bedroom.' He jumped out of bed. 'What?' he shouted. 'Where?' My head was still under the duvet.

'I daren't look,' I cried, 'but he's there just above the bed.'

I can't remember exactly how my husband responded to this. He probably swore, he certainly told me off, then got back into bed, turned over and went back to sleep. The next morning when I reminded him of what had happened, he just laughed, saying I'd probably had a bad dream. 'Maybe,' I said, but I was sure I hadn't been dreaming.

The next night I was really apprehensive about going to bed. I put it off until well after midnight, thinking that if I was really tired I would drop straight off to sleep, and there would be no chance of me waking up until the next morning.

At exactly 3 a.m. the same thing happened. I awoke suddenly and could see the same old man hovering about three feet above the bed. This time I could feel his presence, as well as see him, so I wasted no time in diving under the duvet. When I eventually felt brave enough to take another peek, the apparition had gone.

No matter what I tried, every night that week, the same thing happened at exactly the same time. I couldn't believe it. I was tired and drained, as well as scared and frustrated. I felt overwhelmed by what was happening, and again was desperate for some form of help to alleviate what was turning into a huge problem.

Back into the circle

Deciding that I had no option but to return to the Spiritualist church on Saturday night, I asked my husband if he was still willing to accompany me. He confirmed that he would love to go and find out what all the fuss was about.

This time, the medium was an elderly lady. She was quite plump, and well-spoken. After finishing her second message, she pointed to me. I shrank down in my seat, half-expecting a telling-off from the way she looked at me. The medium told me my grandmother was communicating, and that I had been changing the curtains in my bedroom that day (which I had). She made a bit of a joke and told me that putting up a different set of curtains wouldn't stop me from having some sleepless nights. She said it appeared that I had been having some strange dreams, but in fact the spirit world was trying to make contact – the trouble was that I just wouldn't listen. Everyone laughed at this, and I felt really embarrassed. The medium concluded my message by telling me that my sleepless nights would end if I would only listen to what was being said.

I thought the message was good. I felt proud that my Nana Jackson had come through to speak to me, and I was amazed that the medium seemed to know about the week of sleepless nights I'd had. However, I was somewhat puzzled that she had told me to start listening to the spirit people who were trying to make contact.

The service ended, and we decided not to stay for the open circle. I could also tell that my husband was rather bored with the proceedings, and that he would probably not have taken it too seriously.

Mum rang me again the next morning, to discuss the service. This time, I was in a slightly more positive mood, and I fired questions at Mum, one after another. She laughed at my thirst for information, and suggested that I continue coming along to the church to learn more. I agreed that I would do this, and life fell into a pattern of working part-time during the week, and looking forward to my evenings out at Stephen House on Saturdays. Sometimes my husband accompanied me, but more often than not he went out for a drink with friends.

I got into the habit of talking away to the spirit people in my mind on a regular basis. At this stage, I was not too sure about who my guides and helpers were, so I did not address my thoughts to anyone in particular. I constantly asked for help to understand about Spiritualism, and for assistance in learning more about mediumship.

I continued to sit in the open circle each week, and found that I was often able to give out messages to the other sitters. The main thing I lacked was confidence.

One week, I went to watch a medium who my mum had told me was very good indeed. Her name was Janet Vaughan and she lived in Doncaster. I was impressed with her mediumship during the service, and was thrilled when Mum announced that Janet had agreed to stay behind and sit in the open circle with us. I was keen to hear more of the messages she would undoubtedly deliver.

The circle got under way, and I began passing on messages. I had a really good night; the information was flowing quickly, and I was able to get round quite a few people. My mum also worked well that night, as did Gwynneth. I was quite disappointed, however, because Janet just sat for most of the circle with her eyes closed and her hands folded in her lap. At the end of the circle, as always Gwynneth asked each of us if we had any further messages to pass on. Then she came to Janet, who nodded, stood up, and said, 'Yes – I want to talk to you.' I was surprised to see her pointing at me. I hoped I hadn't done anything to offend her.

'Why aren't you taking church services, young lady?' she boomed.

'I'm not ready,' I replied.

'Nonsense!' she said. 'You're ready. Come and see me at the end of the circle and I'll give you my phone number. If you give me a call I'll be happy to take you round some of the churches that I serve, and I'm sure they'll give you bookings in your own right – you're very good.' And with that she sat down again.

I went to see Janet after the circle, and she kindly did give me her phone number, just as she had promised. However, I didn't consider myself good enough to demonstrate my mediumship publicly at that stage and so I never did ring her. I have since found out that at about the same time as she gave me her phone number, Janet Vaughan was also taking some public meetings with another medium from Doncaster – Paul Norton. I often wonder what would have happened if I had accepted her offer. Would I have met Paul earlier? Would things have been any different?

At that time, however, I lacked knowledge in so many areas, and this affected my confidence. I needed to understand the processes involved in mediumship. I wanted to be more accurate. I yearned for information, but didn't know how to source it.

Healer or medium?

It was around this time that I also became very interested in healing. Before the church service started each week, I would work with the other healers at Stephen House, channelling healing energy into members of the congregation who were ill. Healing appealed to me because it meant I didn't have to stand up in front of an audience, and I could work more on a one-to-one basis.

I have always felt a strong urge to help other people, and to me healing seemed like one of the most useful forms of mediumship. I convinced myself that the ability to ease another person's pain and suffering was far more important than being able to give messages. What I failed to realise at the time was that passing on messages is also an important form of healing, as it often eases emotional pain in a way that hands-on healing cannot.

One lady who came to church, and who suffered from multiple sclerosis, regularly requested that I be allowed to give her some healing. This benefited her so much that she asked if I would be willing to visit her home once a week to give her a bit of extra help. It turned out that she only lived round the corner from my house, and so I agreed.

I used to nip round on a Sunday afternoon, have a bit of a chat with her, and then ask the spirit world to channel their healing energy through me. This worked really well for about five weeks. However, on the sixth week when I went to see her, I had a bit of a problem.

I started the healing process as usual, by closing my eyes, taking some deep breaths and placing my hands on the patient's shoulders. I concentrated really hard, asking the spirit people to work with me. I knew I was in trouble when I suddenly felt very dizzy. I did not feel at all well, and the dizziness became worse and worse. I prayed, asking the spirit people for help, but the dizziness continued. I also felt very nauseous and light-headed, as though I wasn't in control. At that point I began to panic, and my breathing became shallow and rasping. Eventually I collapsed in a heap on the floor. My patient, who was a wheelchair-user, had no option but to wait until I came round, which was apparently quite a few minutes. When I did so, I was naturally embarrassed, but gladly accepted a cup of coffee before I returned home.

Unfortunately, after this incident I declined any further requests for hands-on healing. This was because I hadn't understood what happened that afternoon, and no one seemed able to offer any explanation. Being the stubborn person that I am, I decided I just wouldn't work for the spirit world in that way any more.

As I look back, I wonder if this situation was engineered by my helpers in the spirit world, so that I would rethink my future.

Doubts and fears

Over a period of time I began to feel unsettled about my lack of knowledge and constantly pestered Mum for help and information. Her own understanding was fairly limited, as was Gwynneth's, and they repeatedly informed me that they weren't professional mediums and so weren't qualified to teach me. Their advice was to join a 'development circle' (a kind of teaching group for trainee mediums). However, when I asked where I could find one, they didn't know. I asked if they could start their own development circle within the Spiritualist church at Retford, but they said they needed a professional medium to run it.

Week after week, I asked them to find someone to run a development circle; week after week I was disappointed. I soon discovered that working mediums are often too busy to run circles, and are reluctant to take on this extra work for a church to which they don't belong. Feeling disillusioned, I sent thoughts to the spirit world, asking them to send a qualified medium to the church who would be willing to teach us all. Every night in my prayers I asked for knowledge and understanding, and constantly made it clear to the spirit world that I wasn't prepared to work for them without some positive intervention on their part.

Meanwhile, 20 miles away in Doncaster, Paul Norton was taking the area by storm, with his brilliant demonstrations of mediumship. He had trusted in the spirit world from the beginning, and his faith had been rewarded by many opportunities to practise his gifts. His reputation was growing rapidly. But, in all honesty, even if I had come into contact with him then, I would have been completely in awe of him, and would no doubt have shrunk into the shadows where I felt happiest at that time.

CHAPTER 8
Paul: The evidence speaks for itself

Whilst Tracy was being held back by her lack of confidence, my work was going from strength to strength. However, I still hadn't passed my driving test and, with all the bookings I had accepted, I knew I had to sort this out.

I'd been taking lessons for some time, but as my instructor didn't seem to be in too much of a hurry to put me forward for my test, I decided to book an appointment myself. He wasn't at all impressed and thought I had a lot of work to do before I was ready.

Nevertheless, we were now committed to a date, and to be fair to him he did his best to help me get ready. The day of the test soon arrived and I prayed for the spirit world to help me, emphasising the need for me to pass the test so that I could go wherever I was needed to do their work.

'Right, Mr Norton, I want you to read that registration number on the red car over there,' said the examiner.

I did so without any problems and got behind the wheel. The examiner asked me to start the car and follow his directions. In next to no time we had arrived back at the test centre. I wasn't sure if we had come back so soon because I had done well with my driving, or if it was because I had driven really badly and so had already failed. I knew that the next part of the test involved answering some questions about driving and the Highway Code and was so nervous by this point that my mind went completely blank. I asked my spirit guide Naiomi to help me out.

To my utter surprise, the examiner proceeded to ask me all the questions I was familiar with, and the answers just rolled off my tongue.

'Mr Norton,' he said, 'I'm pleased to inform you that you have passed your driving proficiency test.'

I left the test centre feeling on top of the world and immediately went round to see my friends Sam and Yvonne Corby, who were looking after Daz for me. Sam was a Tarot card reader and often worked alongside a very good friend of mine, medium Janet Vaughan.

As I walked up the path, I could see Janet looking out of the window and so I quickly tried to fake a solemn expression as I walked dejectedly into the house.

'Well,' said Janet excitedly. 'You've done it, haven't you?'

'I've passed,' I said, whilst quite literally jumping up in the air. They all gave me a round of applause.

'I knew you would pass,' said Sam. I discovered many years later that Janet had also encouraged Tracy during the early stages of her development. This would have been another opportunity for us to have met sooner, but it seemed that destiny wasn't yet ready to bring us together.

Joining forces

Sam was a wonderful person and mentor; he taught me a great deal about psychic powers and their use. He was also very comical and used to make me cry with laughter. During those early years, he and Janet helped me many times. Sadly, they have both now passed over. Despite knowing that they live on in the spirit world, I sorely miss their sense of fun and enthusiasm.

It was Sam who suggested that Janet and I should join forces, and I happily asked her to work with me at one of my charity meetings in Doncaster. We arrived at the theatre to discover that most of the tickets had been sold, and we walked out on stage together to the sound of thunderous applause.

Janet spoke first and gave some remarkable messages to the audience. I followed in the second half, and my work was equally well received. Despite our nerves and the worry of working with such a large audience, the evening turned out to be a great success. Afterwards, we spent some time talking to people about the messages they had received.

Sam suggested that we should take some more meetings together. I eagerly agreed, as it had been quite lonely at times, travelling from town to town on my own. Janet was very enthusiastic, and so we organised a small local tour of South Yorkshire.

One of the most memorable meetings we did together was in Rotherham.

Janet went first and she worked very well indeed, delivering around six messages. When I went out in the second half, there was a lovely atmosphere, and whilst I was working, a young girl of 15 made contact with her sister.

'She says it's Carol,' I said. 'Yes,' cried her sister in the audience, 'that's my sister's name.'

'She's taking me to Herring... Herring Road? By the shops, she says. We hit a lamp post – I wasn't supposed to be in the car.'

'It was by the shops on Herringthorpe Road and they did hit a lamp post. She'd only gone out to the chip shop and she was offered a lift. She had been told not to mix with the boys whose car it was,' she replied.

Carol was a very good communicator. At the end of the message, she said to me, 'Will you tell my sister I've got her little boy and he's gorgeous.'

I relayed many similarly touching messages that night and both Janet and I agreed that it had been a great success.

Another event we did together was organised by my good friends Gail and Paul at the local Spiritualist church in Edlington. Over a 100 people were packed into a small community hall.

As usual, Janet wanted to go first. 'I think I'll take my shoes off on the platform, because they're too uncomfortable,' she said, just before the start.

Without realising what I was saying, I replied, 'Oh, don't do that, Janet. I can see you falling.'

'Give over, Paul,' Janet said sternly. 'That's not a very nice thing to say.'

'Well, don't say I didn't warn you,' I quipped.

I decided to watch from the side to see how she got on. Janet started off very well indeed, it all seemed to be flowing very well, and there was a great sense of expectancy in the hall. Halfway through, she said, 'I just feel as if I should step down onto the floor.' With that, she promptly put her foot out to climb down from the platform. As she did so, she literally seemed to shoot across the floor, and under the first row of seats. I burst out laughing, and so did everyone else.

Janet hadn't realised that the floor had been highly polished and so, when she stepped onto it with stockinged feet, it was a bit like walking on an ice-skating rink, resulting in her giving us an impromptu acrobatics display. Fortunately, the only injury she sustained was to her pride.

When it was my turn to work, I sensed a little spirit boy, who wanted to speak.

'He gives me the name of Alan, and I believe this little boy drowned,' I said. A lady sitting at the back put up her hand.

'He must have been about 2 or 3 years old,' I continued.

'Yes, it's my grandson,' the lady replied.

'He climbed through a hole in the fence, and over the backs to the pond. He was playing there and fell in,' I said.

Alan's grandmother confirmed the details, and by this time the audience were listening quite attentively. As each part of the message was relayed, I heard the occasional gasp. Alan went on to give some more family details and information about himself, and at the end of the message he gave me another name.

'He's telling me it's either Davies, or Davidson.' The whole audience gasped, and his grandmother replied, 'His name was Alan Davies.'

I found out after the meeting that, quite a few years previously, Alan Davies had gone missing from his grandmother's house one afternoon. The police were called and the whole village of Edlington co-ordinated a search for him, fearing he had been abducted. As it transpired, Alan was later found in a pond at the back of his grandmother's house. A lot of the people present had remembered the incident, as the village was a very close-knit community.

I have always found that when the need is the greatest, the messages from the spirit world are quite remarkable. That night in Edlington those people created a wonderful atmosphere and the message from Alan Davies, amongst others, helped to convince many of them that there is indeed an afterlife. Many of them had known about Alan's disappearance and had in some way helped in the search for him. Alan had come back, not only to talk to his grandmother, but also to say thank you to all those people who had helped and supported his family whilst he was missing, and after his death became public knowledge.

Positive feedback

I had a lot of church services booked that year and travelled extensively. Janet and I did work together on quite a few occasions over the coming months, but having our own separate commitments meant that we eventually went our own separate ways. However, we did remain very good friends indeed and stayed in touch.

I found that I received lots of requests for one-to-one readings wherever I went, and often received wonderful feedback from people I had spoken to. I was really pleased to receive this particular letter from a lady who originally came from Germany:

Dear Paul,

I first saw you working as a medium in Bridlington where you gave extremely good evidence of survival to a very good friend of mine. That same night, I approached you and arranged to have a private sitting with you.

During this sitting, you produced proof of survival in great detail, which left me beyond any doubt: there is not just a life after death and a very well-informed one about our problems as such, but also a way of communication through mediums like you.

It must have been very difficult for you, as my country of origin is Germany. Many names of relatives and places from my home country were given to me. Here I would just like to mention a few, like my grandmother Olga, with full description, my mother Maria, inclusive detail from her life and items now in my possession; also my uncles Anton, Johann, Hans and Vogt. Places like Oberammergau, Weil, Weinheim and in particular Gutersloh were named. Gutersloh is a small town in Westphalia, where my grandmother's relatives originated from. If you were given a name of a place you could not pronounce, you would spell it, relating to me a recognisable German word.

Repeating your own words, if you can give true proof, help and comfort to only one person, your efforts are worthwhile. I hope you can give this proof to many people.

Ingrid M. Feuchte

This particular sitting for me constituted remarkable evidence. Not only did I not have prior knowledge about Ingrid, but I certainly had no knowledge of Germany and German names.

Another letter, which I received at that time, was from a lady I met in London. I had been invited by Marion Massey (the lady who discovered and managed the singer Lulu) to have tea with Michael Endacott, of the Institute of Complementary Medicine, and herself.

Marion's home was also her office. Her assistant, Patrina Lorden, was asked to join us. During the tea, I sensed that there was something wrong with Patrina. As it turned out she suspected that she had cancer and was naturally very worried whilst she waited for the results of medical tests. I tuned into the spirit world and was able to tell her that she did not have cancer. Here's what she wrote:

Dear Paul,

   It was so wonderful meeting you. Your message came true and I didn't have cancer of the breast. I still have to be checked every six months. You certainly were an inspiration to me.

   I wish you well in your career. I know that you will do well. I hope I'll be able to help you.

   With lots of love from,

                                                                          Patrina

I knew that Patrina was in the clear, but all the same to hear the news confirmed by her was such a relief.

On the air

It wasn't long after Patrina's letter that I received my first invitation to take part in a radio interview. I was booked to appear on Radio York. They'd invited me in to come in and speak to them to help publicise a meeting I was soon to be taking in Scarborough. I arrived at the studio in good time and the reception staff made me very welcome.

About five minutes before the interview I was taken upstairs and introduced to the presenter Kate Kaverner. She was very bright and bubbly, and explained how the interview would be conducted, informing me that she would like to do a phone-in. And then we were live on air!

Kate quickly introduced me and went on to ask about my work. I explained a bit about the spirit world and how a medium works, at which point she interrupted.

'But don't you think that these messages are at times somewhat prosaic?' she asked. 'Like, "Don't leave the iron on or you'll burn your dress"?'

'Prosaic?' What on earth did she mean? I was lost for words, and stuttered my reply. 'Er no, not really.'

'Not even a little bit ordinary?' she persisted.

Oh, so that's what she meant. Now I could answer her.

'Well, you have to remember that these people who communicate are very ordinary people, no different from you or me. They would only mention relevant facts, thoughts and feelings. If a person was forgetful, say for instance with an iron, their loved ones in the spirit world would no doubt mention it, along with anything else which is of importance.' We talked some more about my work and the meeting in Scarborough. Kate then announced that the lines were open for calls.

Everything was happening very quickly. Within a matter of seconds, lots of little red lights started flashing in front of me.

'The lines are jammed, Paul,' said Kate.

I couldn't believe it. We'd only intended to take three or four calls, and now we had several people wanting to ask questions, in the hope of getting a message from the spirit world. Kate's producer suggested that we should take all the calls, but because of the time factor it would be better if we continued off-air. I didn't mind at all, so the producer took me next door to the control room.

One by one, I took each call. Some people were asking about the meeting at Scarborough but most were looking for messages. One lady came on the line who sounded very sad indeed.

'I have a gentleman with me who's giving me the name Rob,' I told her. 'But he's saying Rob and Bob.'

'Yes,' came the lady's reply, 'Rob is my husband and Bob is my son.'

'He's telling me that he passed with cancer, in the stomach.'

'That's true.'

'This must only have been recently. He's showing me the number five – yes, five weeks ago, is that right?'

By this time the lady on the phone was crying uncontrollably. 'Yes,' she sobbed.

'He said it was very quick, all over in a week.'

'He was diagnosed on the Monday,' she said, 'and he passed away the following Monday.'

'Well, he says I'm to tell you that he loves you very much indeed and that he's got Pa and Sid with him.'

'Pa is his dad and Sid is mine,' she said.

'I have to tell you that the house is safe. He says you are not to concern yourself – it is quite safe.' With that the contact just faded and I had to end the message.

Afterwards, the lady explained that her husband's insurance had run out and she was worried about losing the house because she didn't have enough to pay the mortgage. We discovered some time later that the lady's husband's insurance company had agreed to pay as he had only missed one premium and this had been due the week he'd fallen ill.

I think that this was one of the best messages of the day.

Serving others

An important point to note is that the spirit people don't always communicate to us what we want to hear. This often makes it difficult for the medium to know whether they should actually repeat what the spirit person is telling them.

After the Scarborough meeting, I gave a very interesting sitting to one lady who contacted me, asking for help. The lady's mother was communicating with her, but I could sense that there was some kind of barrier between her and her daughter. As I listened carefully to what the mother in the spirit world was telling me to say, I couldn't believe what I was hearing.

'You can tell her I still hate her,' she said.

'Pardon?' I replied out loud. The spirit mother repeated what she'd said. I played for time for several moments until it became almost embarrassing, wondering how on earth I could repeat what I'd heard. By now, the daughter was becoming quite impatient.

'Look,' I said, 'I may be wrong about this, so please forgive me if I am, but I'm sure your mother just said that she still very much dislikes you.'

'Are you sure she said *dislikes?*' came the daughter's abrupt reply.

'Well actually,' I whispered, 'she said she still hates you.'

'And I do her,' came the reply, followed by her bursting into uncontrollable laughter.

As it turned out, the mother and daughter had never got on. In fact, as they both admitted, they really hated each other! The lady told me that many mediums had said her mother was communicating, but that they'd always let themselves down by saying she was sending her love. I'd been the only one who had the guts to repeat what I'd heard. The lady thanked me a great deal because, for her, this was the best evidence she could have received that it really was her mother who was communicating.

The life of a medium is a life of service. We have to try to do what the spirit world expects of us, whilst at the same time providing what the living world wants. Sometimes there is a vast difference in the needs of the two worlds, and we are left stuck in the middle.

However, I personally feel very happy when I am able to help people who really need a contact from the spirit world, and that sense of happiness is greatly enhanced when people take the time to write and let me know how useful my work has been to them.

On another occasion, a lady came to see me, in the hope of receiving a message from her mother. I became frustrated because I knew it wasn't a spirit lady who had come to talk; it was a spirit gentleman who was very much in my thoughts. I began to describe this gentleman to the lady, and explained he had passed away quite recently, following a period in hospital. I described his personality and appearance quite accurately, I thought; that is until the lady told me that this sounded like her husband – but he was still alive! She had come straight from the hospital to my house for her sitting.

In the end, I had to tell the lady that I was sorry but I couldn't continue the meeting with her, as things weren't quite going to plan. She left at around 12.35 p.m. The next day, I was very upset to receive a telephone call from the same lady telling me that her husband had in fact passed away at 12.30 p.m. the previous day – the exact time that I had been describing him to her! This was unbelievable proof that if you are in the right place at the right time, the spirit people will pull out all the stops to let you know they are there!

As well as working in theatres and public meetings it's always nice to be able to help people on a one-to-one basis, particularly when they have lost a loved one and feel so bereft that they cannot carry on. Through private sittings, contact of a personal nature can be and often is achieved.

When a sitting works well, it is an uplifting experience for both the sitter and the medium. The satisfaction of passing on a really good message is tremendous, to say the least. This satisfaction becomes even more profound when people who have had sittings let you know not only that things they were unsure about were correct, but also just how much help to them you have been.

Meeting Annie

Over the years, I have definitely improved my skills as a medium, and this has been confirmed through the wonderful comments and feedback I have received.

Following a service I took at Worksop Spiritualist church, I was approached by a lady named Annie Gloster who enquired if I would see her for a one-to-one meeting. The reading went well, bringing some excellent evidence from Annie's grandmother in the spirit world. Annie sent me this letter a few days later:

Dear Paul,

My grandmother passed to the spirit world just over a year ago, and although I had received messages from her in church, I always felt that these were more like one-way communications as in church they can talk to us, but we rarely get the opportunity to ask them anything.

When I came for my sitting you picked up my gran almost immediately. You got the name Annie, then Anne. Her name was Anne, but like myself, everyone called her Annie. You said that there was a grave with a woman buried on top of a man. This is true: my gran was buried on top of my grandad.

You told me that there is a ring belonging to her and also a locket or something on a chain. The ring is now something I treasure. It was her engagement ring. The thing on a chain is a pocket watch that belonged to my grandad, which was a comfort to her in her years after he passed.

You said she thanked me for the plant. It was a pinkish-purple cyclamen that I'd bought for her birthday and passing anniversary, which are very close together. One of the flowers had snapped off. I put it in a glass of water, and the amazing thing was that the flower lived in that glass in perfect condition for six weeks longer after the plant had withered.

You told me that she'd passed just after Christmas. It was in fact on the 28th December.

I felt that you made my gran 'come to life' by the expressions you used, the intonation of the voice and the same mannerisms, like when you said, 'Will you get that dripping tap fixed.' You said this just like Gran would have done and it got me laughing.

You also said, 'For goodness sake, will you get your teeth checked?' I don't know – this was said in a mock scolding way, and your finger was wagging just like Gran's. You said I'd be going to the dentist between 20th and 28th March. The receptionist gave me an appointment for the 21st!

Through you, Gran told me her eyes and sight are OK now and her hair is beautiful again; also that she no longer has trouble with her feet. All these were things which had troubled her whilst she was on the earth.

She brought back the memory of our little dog Cindy, who was tan in colour and who wagged her tail non-stop. We used to take Cindy up to Gran's bedroom when she was ill. She was such a lively little dog and never failed to cheer Gran up.

I asked Gran through you if I should keep my teeth or have them out. Her reply was to keep what I'd got while I can or they'll be taking me out bit by bit. (I've already lost my tonsils, adenoids and appendix.)

She said I'd been looking at old photographs. I had in fact sorted through a box of old photographs, looking for one of Gran. I could only find tiny ones, so I used several to make up a sort of collage, which I put into a frame.

You gave me the names of relatives accurately. You said that Gran was a very humorous person who could find a funny side to almost any situation. This was very true.

All through the sitting, I laughed along with her and you. It was like the three of us had got together for a natter. The fact that my gran was invisible to me was immaterial. To me she was there and very much alive.

Annie Gloster

The reason Annie had decided to come to see me was because she had been adopted and wanted to find her birth mother. Other mediums had told her that her mother was in fact dead and they had claimed to make contact with her mother's spirit. I didn't get any contact from her mother at all on the day and, given the fact that spirit loved ones are more likely to communicate during sittings, I could only assume that she had not passed over. I strongly felt that Annie would one day find her mother and was given the impression that she lived just outside Birmingham.

Annie later contacted me to let me know that what I had said was in fact correct, and that she had found her mother living just 10 miles outside Birmingham. As a result of this sitting, Annie and I became quite friendly. She introduced me to some of her friends, one of whom was a lady called Joyce, who had spina bifida. We all had great fun together, and for a few months we met on a regular basis to sit in a small home circle, but as usual, I was so busy I found it extremely difficult to juggle all my commitments, and eventually had to close the circle down. Sadly I lost touch with Annie, but I still see Joyce from time to time, and she always gives me a friendly smile and a wave.

CHAPTER 9
Tracy: One step forward, two steps back!

Feeling somewhat disillusioned by the fact that I was unable to find anyone who was qualified to help me to learn more about the work of a medium, I threw myself into my job at the Benefit Office. I had been temporarily promoted and spent most of my days interviewing unemployed people on a one-to-one basis, helping them back to work.

We were often short-staffed, and new people started working at the office on a regular basis. One new member of staff who played an important role in my life was Vanessa. She had just moved into the area with her husband Phillip, who was a medium. Given the fact that I had been asking for help with my spiritual development, I thought the timing of Vanessa's arrival was quite uncanny.

We got on well from the moment we met. During the first week that I knew her, I enjoyed hearing her talk about her own life and beliefs, but I hadn't yet mentioned to her that I was involved in Spiritualism. I was therefore astounded when she told me that she and her husband planned to visit the local Spiritualist church in Retford the following Saturday. She asked if I knew anything about the church, and where it was located. I told her that I knew full well where it was, as my mother was the President.

A chance to get some training

Saturday arrived, and Vanessa and her husband were already at the church when I arrived. After the service I was introduced to Phillip, who was a very pleasant man.

They agreed to stay for the open circle, and I introduced them to Mum and Gwynneth.

Naturally, Mum and I wasted no time asking Phillip about starting a development circle and he eventually agreed to put aside some time for teaching. I was overjoyed at this news and looked forward to finally starting some 'proper' training.

The circle met each week; gradually I learned to meditate, and became more aware of my spirit guides. I also learned how to give psychic messages using psychometry, and a variety of other methods. Phillip was an accomplished and very knowledgeable teacher. I felt it was all going really well, but sadly, after only a few months, he decided to end the circle, as he felt over-burdened with commitments.

Phillip worked full time, served Spiritualist churches, and also ran another development group in Newark – so he didn't have very much time to spare. Luckily for me, I received an invitation to join the Newark Group, and so my training continued.

It wasn't long before Phillip invited me to go and take a service with him at a local Spiritualist church. I didn't feel ready to take this step. However, with a little gentle persuasion from him, I finally agreed.

The big day approached, and I was petrified! I hadn't slept the night before, and hadn't eaten all day, so I felt quite ill by the time I arrived at Phillip's house to begin the journey to the church. He had been booked to take a mid-week service at a Spiritualist church in Chesterfield, and he had already agreed with the president that he could take a novice medium with him.

We arrived in plenty of time and around 30 people were already waiting eagerly for the service to begin. All too soon, we were being led into the main area of the church, and up onto the platform. This was it. My work as a medium was about to begin. My hands were shaking, my knees were trembling and I wasn't sure I could go through with it, but I didn't want to let Phillip down so I tried really hard to compose myself.

In no time at all, Phillip had finished his prayer and talk, and it was my turn to stand up. I don't remember very much about what I did, although I do recall pointing to a woman in the middle of the room, and giving her a message from her father, which brought her to tears. After this the messages came very easily, despite my obvious nerves. Eventually, when I felt I could do no more, I turned to Phillip to ask him to continue. He merely smiled enigmatically, and pointed out that it was time for the service to end. I sat down exhausted, pleased that it was all over, but elated that I had done it. This was a real achievement for me, as I still lacked confidence, and needed constant reassurance and encouragement about my work. I couldn't believe that I had actually stood up in front of people and given messages from the spirit world – maybe I could be a medium after all!

After the service had ended, we were given a cup of tea, and I was approached by the booking secretary to see if I would take a service of my own. I politely declined, telling her that I wasn't taking bookings of my own at that point.

On the journey home, Phillip told me he was very happy with what I had done, and gave me plenty of constructive criticism and advice. He offered to take me to another church service he had booked the following week. Because I was comfortable in the knowledge that Phillip would be there to help and support me, I immediately agreed.

A difficult experience

The next booking was on a Sunday at Mansfield. We agreed on the way there that Phillip would say the prayers and do the philosophy, and I would then start with the messages. I delivered fewer messages that night, and allowed Phillip to take over halfway through. However, I was still pleased with the way it had gone, and my confidence was coming on in leaps and bounds. Once again, I was approached by the booking secretary with an invitation to take a service on my own – once again I declined. I felt I needed a bit more practice first.

A few weeks later, I was invited to accompany Phillip again, this time to Sutton in Ashfield. I was given a lovely warm welcome by the church president and, whilst Phillip was giving his talk, I prepared myself to work by welcoming my spirit guides, and asking for their help. It was soon my turn to speak, and I began to deliver messages to different people around the room. I was doing really well, until I pointed to a young man at the back and told him I had a message for him from his grandmother in the spirit world. He immediately folded his arms and wouldn't respond to the information I was giving him. I couldn't understand why this was, as I was certain that what I was saying was right, but he just wouldn't accept any of it. Eventually I became quite upset by this, and asked Phillip to take over. As I sat down, I couldn't hold back my tears. I felt humiliated and I was angry at the spirit world for allowing me to be shown up in this way. The service ended, and Phillip handed me his handkerchief. The church president approached and told me I had done really well, but I was inconsolable, determined that I wouldn't put myself through this again.

On the way home, Phillip tried to reassure me that it was the young man who had been receiving the message who was at fault and not me. I couldn't understand at that time, that audience members can affect the work of mediums and, as is my nature, I blamed myself. Despite Phillip's attempts to comfort and reassure me, I made it quite clear that I didn't want to work as a medium ever again. Phillip, however, had other ideas, and he rang me the next day to say that he had accepted a booking on my behalf to work at a Special Evening of Mediumship at the church in Newark. He told me it was important that I accept this booking, as it would help the church president to see how well the development group was going, and it would help me to get my confidence back. Although I agreed on the phone, I had absolutely no intention of going along and doing the evening. I decided that I would think of some suitable excuse nearer the time.

However, the night approached, and I felt guilty about letting myself down, as well as Phillip and the church, but most of all the spirit people who had given me this wonderful opportunity. When we arrived at the church I began to wish I hadn't agreed, for it was a much larger audience than I had expected, with around a hundred people waiting to receive messages. I met the other mediums, who were lovely, and who reassured me that I would be fine, and that if I had any problems they would take over.

I passed on three messages that night, and worked really well. I remember pointing a woman out at the back of the church and giving her a message from her mother. It had everyone giggling as I proceeded to describe her mother watching over her that morning whilst she had been moving the furniture round in her bedroom, and had spent ages cleaning up the fluff from under her bed. I described the exact new positioning of the furniture in the room, and told her about the new curtains she had put up at the window.

My final message was to a lady in the middle of the room from her father, who had passed with throat cancer. I came a little bit unstuck during this message, as I could really feel the sensation of the cancer in my throat, and began to find it difficult to speak. As a result I had to ask Phillip to intervene, which he did, but he only took over for a short while, until I was more composed, and then he allowed me to finish the message off for myself. I sat down, tired but happy that I had been brave enough to have another go at working as a medium in public.

Taking a break from mediumship

I had found the whole experience of appearing as a medium in public quite draining, and I still wasn't sure if it was the right thing for me to do. I questioned this even further when, soon after the Special Evening at Newark, I found out that I had been promoted, and I was offered a job at Mansfield Jobcentre. This job was full-time. With the extra travelling involved, it would take up a lot more of my day than my part-time job in Retford had.

I knew that, if I accepted this job, it was unlikely that I would be able to continue my spiritual work, and so, after a great deal of careful thought, I decided to accept the post and give up Spiritualism altogether. I really felt that this was the best thing to do, as I wanted to spend more time with Gemma and my husband, and knew that I couldn't possibly do this if I had a full-time job as well as church bookings. I was also finding my spiritual work very stressful, and, although I seemed to have a wonderful gift, I did not feel strong enough in myself to put it to good use.

Not long afterwards, I also lost contact with Phillip and Vanessa, so it seemed that the time wasn't quite right for me to pursue a spiritual pathway at that point. Other things were to happen in my life at that time which further confirmed to me that I had made the right decision. It seemed that my career as a medium was over before it had really had a chance to begin. Maybe I had known it wouldn't work out all along, which was why I had been so reluctant to do the work from the beginning!

Working at the Jobcentre in Mansfield was totally different from working in Retford. The pace was much faster, and the customers more demanding. Having said all this, I enjoyed every minute of working there, and made some wonderful friends.

Even though I no longer went to church, I was still aware of the spirit world around me, and often sensed spirit presences whilst interviewing customers at the Benefit Office. I also had very vivid dreams, which involved family members who had passed to the spirit world, and I was often visited by my Nana or Grandad Jackson (my dad's parents) in this way.

I remember one dream, which I found very uplifting, and which sticks in my mind to this day. It was the night before my birthday, and I was a little bit down as no special plans had been made for 'the big day'.

I dreamed that my Grandad Charlie came to the side of my bed, and gently woke me up. He gave me a hug and a kiss, and told me he had brought my two babies from the spirit world to meet me, and wish me Happy Birthday. He placed two little boys in my arms, who reached out and hugged me, their little faces lit up with huge smiles, their eyes alight with love. Grandad told me that my boys were with him in the spirit world. They stayed with me for a while, and then quite suddenly they were gone. I am convinced that, somehow, my babies came to me in a dream, and will never forget the wonderful feeling I had for days and weeks afterwards.

It was also around this time that we managed to sell the house at Moorgate, and I felt that I could now close the door on that particular episode in our lives. I was convinced that leaving that house would end all links with Spiritualism for good. We bought a semi-detached house on the outskirts of

I was a little bit run down, so you can imagine my surprise when the doctor told me that I was two months' pregnant!

I wasn't sure whether this was a good thing or not. I hadn't been trying to conceive, and had always assumed that Gemma would be an only child. My marriage was not all I had hoped it would be, and there had been quite a few rocky patches along the way. I had been carefully taking the oral contraceptive pill, and couldn't understand how I had become pregnant.

It took me a while to become accustomed to the idea of a new baby. But one thing was certain: I wouldn't be able to continue travelling backwards and forwards to Mansfield each week, and I needed to get a job nearer to home. I was being closely monitored by my midwife and GP because of my previous miscarriages, and was having hormone injections into my spine again to ensure the normal growth of the foetus.

I successfully applied for a job as an adjudication officer, in Newark. I absolutely hated working there. There were about 20 of us in an office, and we had no contact with the general public whatsoever. This was so that the decisions we made relating to benefit were totally independent and objective.

I worked until I was eight months' pregnant, then spent a leisurely month at home preparing for the birth of my second baby. I went into labour exactly on the due date, and gave birth to a whopping 10lb 6oz baby boy, whom we called Luke. Everyone adored him from the minute he was born, as he had such a pleasant, placid nature.

The calm before the storm

I was allowed to take Luke home the next day, and the usual round of midwife's visits, post-natal check-ups, and visits from well-wishers took up most of my time during the first week. Luke seemed to sleep a lot of the time, which I assumed was his nature, but I started to become concerned during our second week at home, when he developed the sniffles and a bit of a cough. I raised my concerns with the midwife, who was also a bit worried, as he didn't seem to be gaining weight. She advised me to make an appointment at the doctor's, which I did, but was told to go home, keep him cool, and make sure he drank plenty of cool boiled water. I was assured there was no real cause for concern.

Luke's health didn't improve, and I made a further two appointments at the doctor's to get him checked out. Both times I was told there was nothing wrong and to go home and get some rest. They must have thought I was just an over-anxious mother, because they really would not take my concerns seriously.

I was getting no sleep at all, as each night Luke's breathing was exceptionally poor, and he needed to be propped up; otherwise he made a weird grating sound within his throat and chest as he gasped for breath. My mum was brilliant, and came round night after night to sit up with Luke so I could get some rest. I didn't sleep much, though. Instead, I chatted with Mum, and together we worried over my baby's health. For the first time in many months I sent out thoughts to the spirit world asking for their help and guidance. One night, completely exhausted, I drifted off to sleep, and was filled with a strange sense of peace. I dreamed that one of my guides from the spirit world, Sister Josephine who worked with me when I was healing, came to sit with me and held my hands.

I remember asking for help for my son, and begging for the healing power to be sent to him, to make him get better. I instinctively knew that he was very ill indeed.

She told me that Luke needed to go to the doctor's one more time, and that this would help to sort matters out. I must continue to pray for him, she said, and to imagine every ounce of motherly love I had passing from my strong, healthy body into his weak, tiny frame. I woke up with a start.

As soon as the doctor's surgery opened, I made an urgent appointment. This time, I was determined to get some answers.

I took Luke in, undressed him, and laid him on the examining table. He was really miserable; his little face was red, and his nose and eyes were blocked with mucus. I wasn't surprised when the doctor told me she felt it would be best if he was admitted to hospital for observation.

I rang my husband, and he agreed to meet me at the hospital. It took about 20 minutes to get there, and we were soon being ushered into a side ward in the paediatric wing. A doctor came immediately to examine Luke, and told us that he had quite a severe chest infection, but they needed to do some tests to ascertain exactly what they were dealing with. They were also concerned that he wasn't feeding, and wanted to try to get him to have something as a matter of urgency. He asked me to sign a consent form for them to insert a tube through Luke's nose and down his throat, which would be used to make sure that he was fed properly.

Luke was then placed in an incubator to ensure that he was breathing in enough oxygen. There was a drip attached to one of his little arms, and a tube pushed up his nose and into his throat. A nurse came in to explain what was happening, and to tell us that from time to time we could put our hand into the incubator to touch him. She advised us to keep talking to him, as he was fully aware that we were there, and it would put him at his ease to know that he wasn't in a strange place alone. A bed was made up in the room, and we were told that one or both of us could stay. I agreed that I would stay with him, and that my husband would go home to see to Gemma, and of course he had to go to work as well.

That night, I dreamed that Grandad Carter, who had died the year before, came to visit us. He stood by the incubator, and exclaimed at how beautiful Luke was. He reached out his hand and placed it on Luke's forehead, whilst looking directly at me with his twinkly blue eyes, 'He's going to be fine, you know,' he said gently. 'You'll be taking him home in a week.' With this, he was gone. I awoke immediately following the dream, and felt peaceful and relaxed. Somehow, I knew that everything was going to be all right, and that I had no need to worry further.

The next morning, there was a slight improvement in Luke's condition, although he was still receiving a great deal of attention and monitoring from the doctors and nurses. After we had been there for three days, he was a lot better, and the nurses wanted me to become more involved in his care, so I was taught how to pour the milk down the tube into his throat, and how to change the tube to avoid infection. After five days, the tube was removed and I was encouraged to try bottle-feeding again. Luke was slightly lazy to begin with, but made good progress, and exactly seven days after he had been admitted, he was given a clean bill of health, and it was agreed I could take him home. Good old Grandad! What he had told me came perfectly true, and I was sure that Grandad and the spirit world had helped Luke in a miraculous way.

A very lucky escape

Life gradually got back to normal. I returned to work, and Mum took over looking after Luke, as well as Gemma. I had been allowed to go back to working part-time, so the strain wasn't too bad, but I still really hated the job in Newark, and yearned for something more challenging, where I would have a chance to work with the general public once again.

Whilst I was still working at Newark, I had a really hair-raising experience, and I am certain the spirit people inter-vened to help me, and save me from harm. I always make people laugh when I recall this story, because they can't believe my stupidity at the time.

One morning, when Luke was about six months old, I was driving to work along the A1 from Retford to Newark. As usual I had my foot down and was speeding along much faster than I should have been. Halfway there I got stuck behind a lorry. I decided to overtake but was shocked to find that, as I tried to pull out, I had no acceleration, and the car just started dropping further behind. I tried to move back into the left-hand lane when I noticed that the fuel gauge was falling dramatically – somehow the car was losing petrol.

I decided to pull over, but as I manoeuvred the car into

the left-hand lane, I was exasperated to find that the brake pedal was hanging off, and was not working at all. By this time I realised I had serious problems. Somehow I managed to get the car on to the grass verge beside the A1. As I pulled up at the side of the road, I noticed an articulated lorry pull up behind me, and was then shocked to see a truck also pull up in front of me, and two young men run towards my car, shouting for me to get out. One of them ran forward, opened my door and grabbed me, physically lifting me out of the vehicle. 'Get out!' he shouted. 'The car's on fire!'

Within seconds of him hauling me out of the vehicle, it burst into flames, and exploded inside. He pushed me to safety on the grass verge, and then he and his friend proceeded to throw buckets of water onto the fire, from a stream at the side of the road. The driver of the articulated lorry approached me and offered to take me to the garage a bit further up the road, so we could call the police and the fire brigade.

I couldn't believe what a lucky escape I had had, and it is at times like this that you really feel as though you are being watched over from above. I don't know what would have happened if I hadn't tried to pull over when I did, and if those two brave young men hadn't approached the car to get me out. Later I learned that I had driven along the A1 for about ten miles with the whole undercarriage of my car on fire – and I hadn't known a thing about it!

A new start

Shortly after this, I got a new job as a disability employment adviser. This job involved managing a caseload of disabled clients, carrying out assessments and working closely with employers in the community to create strategies for getting these people back to work. I had never worked with disabled people before, but the job really suited me, as I felt I was doing something worthwhile with my life, and that I was making a real difference to the lives of some severely disadvantaged individuals. Over the next few months I came into contact with some pretty amazing people whose drive and determination to succeed both humbled me and inspired me to do well in this job. How strange that Paul already worked with someone who was disabled – his good friend Daz. Even more peculiar was the fact that in the future I would be called upon to assist with Daz's care. Maybe the spirit world was ensuring that I received the training they thought was necessary at the time, and not the training I believed I needed!

Initially I was sent back to work at the Benefit Office in Retford, as I was still only part-time and this was a good place for me to train in my new role; but I really loved this job, and was soon working full-time again. I was achieving good results, and had made some good friends, but the long hours meant that I didn't get to spend much time with my family. I was under a considerable amount of stress, my marriage was close to collapse and events over the coming months would tear me away from my job once and for all. It seemed I had no choice in the matter; the spirit world was growing impatient!

CHAPTER 10
Paul: Friends and co-workers

Margaret Pickering, a psychic I'd met a couple of years before, telephoned me quite out of the blue to ask if I would be interested in taking part in a week-long tour of Scotland with herself and another medium, Irene Williams. I'd never been to that part of the country before so the opportunity was too good to miss. I arranged for Daz to stay with friends, and Irene and I decided to meet at the railway station to journey to Glasgow together. We were to stay at a small hotel in the city centre and would use this as our base during our stay in Scotland.

My first impression of Glasgow was that it was a very busy city and, even though I'd passed my driving test some time ago, I hadn't built up the confidence to travel there by car. When I saw the amount of traffic, I was glad I had made the journey by train.

After settling myself into my room, I thought I'd relax for a while and watch some television, after which I intended to have a little chat with the spirit world in preparation for my work that night. I was beginning to feel tired when suddenly I felt a presence in the room. Then, out of the corner of my eye, I saw the outline of a young boy.

'Hello Paul, I'm Alistair,' the lad announced with a very big grin, 'and my Aunty Barbara is coming to see you tonight!'

I was quite shocked by this impromptu apparition, and didn't dare move too much in case he disappeared.

'How did you pass over to the spirit world, Alistair?' I asked him, to check that this was really happening.

'I got an infection in me kidneys,' he replied, 'I'm nine and a half years old.'

I smiled at this and said, 'Well, all right then, will you come and tell me some more about yourself tonight?' Alistair agreed that he would, and almost as quickly as he'd arrived, he disappeared.

An emotional meeting

That evening, we were due to take our first meeting at the Freemasons Hall in Edinburgh and Margaret demonstrated first. The advertisements had apparently asked people to bring photographs and other items along so that they could be 'read' by Margaret and Irene. They demonstrated psychometry, which is where a psychic holds an object and goes on to talk about either its origin or the background of the person to whom the object belonged.

As I stepped out to work in the second half, I immediately noticed a spirit person standing beside a gentleman sitting right at the back of the hall. I pointed towards him and launched into the first message.

'I have a young man here who tells me he passed in an accident. He says he was riding a motorbike.'

'That's my son,' said the man.

'I'm hearing a name, it sounds like Peter,' I continued.

'That's his name,' the man confirmed.

'I'm not quite sure,' I went on, 'but he seems to be about 17 years old.'

'He was 17,' came the man's rather emotional reply.

Peter went on to tell his father that he had seen his mother wearing his watch and his rugby shirt. He told me, 'She was in my room the other day, Sunday.' I relayed this to his father.

'Yes, that's quite true,' he said. Peter told us more about himself and his family. He was a very good communicator, but as time went on, I realised that I needed to end the message as another contact from the spirit world was trying to come through. There was nothing there at first, then I heard a familiar voice.

'Aunty Barbara is sitting over there.' It was Alistair. This time he seemed much stronger and clearer in his communication.

He guided my thoughts towards a lady who appeared to be alone and sitting about halfway down the hall. I looked over towards her; I pointed and said, 'The lady in the white coat.' She looked up, 'Yes, you, my love,' I continued. 'Do you, by any chance, know Alistair in the spirit world?'

'Why yes,' she replied, sounding quite surprised.

'Then you must be his aunty, his dad's sister?' I asked.

'I am,' she answered.

'I have Alistair with me,' I said. 'In fact, he came to me this afternoon whilst I was in my hotel room. He tells me that he got an infection in his kidneys – is that correct?'

'Yes,' came her reply, as she wiped a tear away from her eye. 'He died with kidney failure.'

'He says hello, Barbara.'

With this, Barbara just burst into tears. Alistair went on to tell his aunty that his dad was supposed to come along tonight but at the last minute he had had to cancel because of work commitments. He also told her that he had her dog with him. Barbara was very pleased indeed.

Alistair told me that he was named after his dad; this was confirmed to be true. Towards the end of the message, the young lad reminded me to tell his Aunty Barbara how old he was. I said to her, 'When I was in my hotel room this afternoon, Alistair told me that he is nine and a half.'

Barbara gasped as I relayed this piece of information. 'Alistair passed away two days after he was nine and a half,' she said. 'Whilst he was ill he kept telling everyone how old he was.'

That night's show turned out to be a very emotional and enjoyable meeting indeed. Over 400 people had packed into the Freemasons Hall for our first event in Scotland.

More moving messages

The following evening we were in Perth, then on to Motherwell. Both shows went very well and were equally well attended.

The next stop was Galashiels and the Volunteer Hall was packed to capacity. Irene went before me, demonstrating psychometry once again. When it was my turn, I was immediately drawn to a woman at the back of the hall, who was wearing a red coat.

'I have a little boy with me who has blond hair and blue

eyes,' I told her. 'He tells me he wants to speak to Pat. Is that your name?'

'Yes,' she replied.

'Then who is Ian?' I asked. 'Ian is my little boy who died,' she said.

'Well, he's here talking to me now. Did he pass over with some kind of... hole in the heart?'

'Yes,' she responded, enthusiastically.

Ian was able to tell us many things, including the fact that his mother had had a fire engine made out of some flowers placed on his coffin. She'd also placed a photograph of the family in his little hands.

'I didn't want him to go alone,' she explained. By this point, most of the audience, and even I, were starting to feel quite emotional.

'Well, I can let you know that Ian is with his grandfather, and he is not alone – so you needn't worry any more. I can also tell you that it's your strong love for your son that has helped him to come and talk to us all tonight.' It was a very loving and touching message for me to give, and needless to say Pat was overcome with joy.

Another lady's mother communicated to her. I could see the mother sitting in a wheelchair. She told me that she could propel herself and walk a bit, but she actually preferred someone else to do it for her whenever possible. This caused quite a bit of laughter when I told the audience, especially when her daughter added, 'Aye, she was an idle so-and-so!' The mother in the spirit world agreed. The meeting continued with a great deal of warmth and humour. We'd all worked hard to deliver a unique demonstration.

Glasgow was our final meeting of the Scottish tour and was to be held at the Central Hotel. The promoters suspected that it was going to be a good turn-out and quite rightly so. Nearly 500 people were crammed into the ballroom.

By the time everyone had been seated, it was 7.50 p.m., and we were very late starting – we should have begun at 7.30.

Eventually, it was my turn. I stepped onto the platform and immediately felt the presence of a young man. He told me he'd taken a drugs overdose. 'Kevin's my name,' he said. 'Karen's my sister's best friend.' At this point, I was guided to a young lady sitting near the front of the audience. She had her head bowed.

'I have someone here called Kevin,' I announced. 'I think he wants to speak to you. Are you Karen?' The young lady just looked at me and nodded. As she lifted her head, I could plainly see the pain in her eyes, and that she was really suffering. I described Kevin's passing to her.

'He says it happened in London. He was living alone. He says it was a very small dingy bed-sit.' Karen nodded in agreement. She must have been so very distraught, as she really found it difficult to speak.

'It's not her fault,' Kevin told me. 'Tell her not to blame herself.' I relayed this information to Karen and she couldn't contain herself any longer. Tears were rolling down her cheeks, as she confirmed that what I was saying was correct.

At the end of the meeting, I made my way towards Karen, and put my arm around her. Still sobbing, she told me what had happened. Both Kevin and herself had been drug users. She was supposed to go and visit him in London and take some drugs with her. For one reason or another, she was unable to go.

By that time, Kevin was desperate. He'd apparently concocted his own drug by using sleeping tablets. He'd injected so much into himself, it had caused him to have liver failure. Karen, although beside herself with grief, did say that she felt much better after hearing from Kevin.

The Glasgow show had been the perfect end to a wonderful week. I had never encountered such warm and responsive groups of people as these. I was a little sad when it was time to leave, but I was also looking forward to getting home again.

Working with other mediums

Over the years I have worked with a variety of different mediums, all with their own personalities and ideas. I have already mentioned the wonderful Janet Vaughan, who brought much humour and fun to the work we did together. She had such a wonderful manner that she was able to pass on numerous lovely messages of comfort over many years. Although we didn't work together for a great length of time, Janet's experience no doubt brushed off on me, and helped me to develop and mature.

Another interesting person I worked with was the down-to-earth and straight-talking Sue Cunningham. Sue is well-known around Yorkshire where she lives, and she now travels around the country doing demonstrations of her own. She was also a very fun-loving character, and we shared some very successful demonstrations. Like Janet, Sue was a laugh a minute to work with. I am pleased to hear that Sue is doing well now in her own right. She is a very good medium and has earned her current success.

I also teamed up for a short time with a psychic artist called Haydn Clark. On one occasion we were at the Civic Hall in Barnsley. Because of the size of the hall and the packed audience, Haydn had decided to use an overhead projector. As he put pen to paper, the first picture built up quite nicely and the contact was very good.

I could make out the features quite clearly and it soon became apparent that the portrait was of a man in his late sixties. Turning to look at the audience, I felt compelled to speak to a man who was sitting on the second row.

'I'm getting the name of Hutchinson – William Hutchinson and he seems to be connected with your father. Is this right?' The man nodded in agreement. 'This gentleman,' I said, pointing towards the picture on the screen, 'is part of the same family.'

'Yes,' replied the man. 'William Hutchinson is my uncle, my father's brother, and the picture being drawn is that of my father.'

'Your father passed away with chest trouble – emphysema, I think – because he worked where there was a lot of dust.'

'Yes, that's correct,' came the man's reply.

'He is talking about living in Park Street, in the third house along the left from the alleyway.'

'Yes, that's right.'

'The house and the street no longer exist.' By this time, the man couldn't believe his ears, since the message he was receiving and the image of his father projected on the screen were so accurate. His father in the spirit world gave a very evidential message and offered some practical help with his son's life.

There was also a lady who received a very clear and precise message from her father that night. He was able to tell her that he'd been listening in to her conversation.

'She's had that blue and grey box out again,' her father told me. 'The one with the old photos in. She also took out that big newspaper cutting.'

The lady was quite surprised at what she was being told. Her father continued his message: 'She spoke on the phone to her friend about the box, the pictures and the paper cutting.' The lady confirmed that all this was quite correct.

Another young man communicated to his girlfriend. He had been killed in a car accident. 'We went out of control and hit a tree,' he told me, adding, 'It wasn't our car – we borrowed it, if you know what I mean.'

His girlfriend laughed. 'He means he stole it,' she said. He then showed me a tattoo that he had on his left arm. It was a shield with a name written on it. I described this to his girlfriend, and she nodded tearfully. 'It looks like the name Tracey,' I said.

'Yes,' she whispered. 'That's right, it's me.'

Haydn and I were both really pleased that the evening had been a great success. After the meeting, many people came up to ask about private sittings and wanted to know where and when we would next be appearing.

A great honour

Much to my surprise, in 1994, I was asked by Tim Haigh, Editor of the *Psychic News*, if I would like to work at an event to be held at the Lewisham Theatre in South

London. I was delighted by this invitation and immediately accepted.

In the weeks leading up to it, large advertisements started to appear, publicising the day and listing the mediums who would be taking part. I learned that I would be working alongside such stars as Doris Collins, and the highly respected medium Albert Best. Amongst the younger up-and-coming mediums would be myself, and the now extremely famous Colin Fry.

I was really excited to be part of such a prestigious event and so pleased that the lovely Doris Collins was to be there. After all, she had figured quite a lot in the spiritual path I had taken, and I thought it was rather uncanny that our paths should cross again.

Because I'd worked with Haydn quite successfully in the past, I thought it would be nice for him to come along on the day. The event started at 11 a.m. and we were the first to appear.

I said a very quick good morning, and moved straight into the first message. The contacts from the spirit world came through very smoothly indeed, and Haydn's drawings were well received.

Our spot had gone down really well with the audience, and I was pleased to have been first, because it had given me the opportunity to sit amongst the audience and enjoy the rest of the day. It was nice to be part of an event where so many people were working together for the same cause.

A couple of weeks later the *Psychic News* wrote various articles about those of us who had appeared at Lewisham. The headline for the article about Haydn and myself was

'Clairvoyant and Psychic Artist Leave Audience Breathless'. There was also an article about Albert Best, who had received the Spiritualist of the Year award that day. The people who took part in that event have now all dispersed in different directions. Sadly, Albert and Doris have passed over to the spirit world themselves.

As with so many of the other mediums I had worked with, Haydn and I also eventually went our separate ways. This was predominantly because we lived at different ends of the country. Because our work involved a great deal of travelling anyway, it was just too difficult to arrange bookings to suit us both.

A disillusioning experience

Over the years I have worked as a medium I have had some wonderful experiences working with other mediums, but also some very difficult times – when I have called into question my own judgement of people and their motives. I must admit after the next episode I vowed I would never work with another medium again. Little did I realise that in the future a certain Tracy Hall would appear on the horizon.

This unpleasant experience started when I was approached by a young male medium, who complimented me on my work, and told me all about his own mediumship. As I have said before, I very much like working with other mediums as it does take some of the pressure away, and makes it a more enjoyable experience overall – so I asked this young man if he would like to join me on a couple of demonstrations. In the beginning, all appeared to be going well. Then I realised that he was very 'money-orientated', and all he was interested in was his share of the takings, whilst doing very little in return. The partnership eventually turned sour, when I discovered that the medium in question was 'stealing' my venues behind my back and booking them for himself. He also took my ideas for advertisements, and copied some leaflets I had designed.

The final straw came when I suspected him of having a plant in the audience at a theatre in Nottinghamshire. Although I had had a really good night and given some excellent messages, he was really struggling to make any kind of link, either with the spirit world or the audience. I continued to work myself, but, just as the show was about to end, he stood up and said he wanted to give one more message.

He proceeded to try to place the message in a specific area of the audience. As it turned out, the person he wanted to speak to had moved during the interval to the other side of the room! However, she put her hand up and announced to the audience that she had previously been sitting right where he had originally pointed. He went on to give an outstanding message to the woman, with some pretty astonishing evidence. However, apparently he had previously received a letter from this woman, detailing everything that had been said in the message, and she followed him round from venue to venue! Tracy's mum Janice was in the theatre that night and she vows to this day that the woman was planted to make that medium look good.

News from the family at last

Many people think that being a medium gives you all the answers and constant access to messages from the spirit world, not only for other people but also for yourself. Sadly, this is not the case. Just because we are able to communicate with the spirit world doesn't mean we are able to get in touch with our own family members on a regular basis. Also, sometimes, just because there are lessons to be learned, it doesn't mean to say that the spirit world will step in and save us from making mistakes.

At times, I became disillusioned with my work, as I never seemed to get any messages from my own loved ones in the spirit world – all I ever received were messages about my work. In fact it was many years before I received any contact from my father who, as I mentioned earlier, had taken his own life following a bout of depression.

At the time, I was on my way to Hastings. I had been invited to take part in a Mind, Body and Spirit festival, which was being held there. I was enjoying the views from the train, and glancing at my newspaper, when my eyes started to flicker as the train rocked from side to side. I'd had a good night's sleep so there was no reason for me to feel tired, yet I began to feel extremely drowsy.

Just as I was nodding off, I experienced a sudden jerk, as if I was being yanked from my seat. I felt as if I had been lifted out of my body, and sure enough, I could see myself sitting there on the train. I was in an elevated position, a few feet above where my sleepy body was resting. I seemed to start floating up out of my seat and towards the clouds. As I looked down, I could see the train disappearing beneath me. I can only describe what was happening as an 'out-of-body' experience. I felt slightly perturbed and so decided to send a thought out to see if Naiomi could help me.

'Don't worry,' she advised. 'This is what you want; it has been planned for some time.'

Before she had a chance to go on, another voice interrupted the conversation, shouting urgently, 'Paul, Paul?'

I knew straightaway who it belonged to. As I looked ahead of me I could see the faint outline of a person with a dog standing by his side. It was my dad Peter.

'Paul,' he said, 'I've waited so long to be able to talk to you like this.'

Whilst he was talking the dog came to sit by my side. It was Jackie, my dad's dog. I didn't know her because she'd passed over before I was born. She still had her beautiful black coat, though, the one I'd seen in photos of her. I crouched down and patted her on the back. She jumped up to give my face a lick. Her tail was wagging furiously.

'Are you happy, Dad?' I asked, with a lump in my throat.

'Much happier than I was before,' he replied. 'It took me some time to understand what went wrong. I was helped by Gran when I got over here, and I've since met up with Paul as well.'

'How is he, Dad?' I asked.

'At the beginning he told me he was angry. If the lights had been on red, he said he might have been in with a chance. As time has passed he's gradually come to terms with everything. He's with his grandad now.'

Paul, of course, was the family friend who had been killed in an accident. One thing I never mentioned when I wrote about that incident was that there were some traffic lights and a bridge just before the bend where Paul died. Apparently a number of people had said that if the lights had been on red, it was possible he might have survived.

'Dad,' I said, 'what about Nan? Have you seen her? It was awful, what happened to her, wasn't it?'

'She didn't feel anything, Paul. I know she could see what was going to happen, but you must believe me, it was all so quick. She's sometimes with your grandad.'

'*Sometimes?*' I asked.

'Well, they still don't get on too well,' he added. 'Dad will see her, but he doesn't want her around him all of the time.'

I laughed at this. 'That pair never change, do they?' I commented. I really couldn't believe what was happening. Was I dreaming or was this for real? There was no reason for me to just suddenly fall asleep, and then dream all of this.

'It's for real,' Dad said. 'I can see what you're thinking, as clearly as you can see me.'

There were so many things I wanted to say and ask, but for some reason my mind went completely blank. Sadly, I was just beginning to get used to the idea of being with Dad in this way, when my eyes started to feel heavy again, and I felt Naiomi gently interrupt my thoughts.

'It's time to go,' she commanded.

I couldn't believe this. 'No, no – not yet!' I cried. There was a sudden jolt and I found myself sitting back in the train carriage. In the distance, I could just hear Dad's voice.

'Bye, Son, bye.'

Naiomi leaned towards me, and whispered, 'Just remember how he looked.'

It dawned on me a few seconds later what she meant. Dad had somehow looked different, younger, and without the worry and age lines. Of course I realised that he would look younger simply because he didn't have a physical body. If I'd been dreaming, he would have looked like he did the last time I saw him, drawn and tired. I started to feel elated: I'd really visited Dad. How marvellous!

It all becomes clear

I had spent years waiting for this, going to Spiritualist churches, joining a development circle, and hoping my father would make contact. Finally, the spirits had made it possible. I couldn't thank Naiomi enough. She went on to tell me something interesting.

'If you had been granted your wish in the beginning,' she said, 'you would not have followed the same pathway. You might have done so for a short time, but we had to make sure that you followed your life plan according to the way which was right for you.'

Suddenly it all became clear. The spirit world had had everything planned. I had been stumbling along, often blindly walking into situations, without having a clue that in reality everything had been taking place for a reason: all these events, taken together, had encouraged me to work as a medium.

On reflection, I knew Naiomi was right. If I hadn't wanted something for myself so badly, I probably wouldn't have followed this pathway to the extent that I had. Often I had felt that I had missed out on some of my youth by becoming a medium. I didn't get the chance to go out and socialise, other than with Daz or people who were involved in Spiritualism. I had given up any thought of settling down and having a family, as having a disabled person to look after and being a medium meant that I wasn't really one of the world's most eligible bachelors! I often felt that I had quite a lonely life, and it wasn't necessarily the life I would have wanted for myself.

The spirit people had obviously thought that I would help their cause, and so they ensured that I followed the way they knew was right. All these thoughts went round in my head on the rest of the journey.

Age before youth?

The Mind, Body and Spirit Festival in Hastings was well attended. The venue was alive with the sound of voices and music. I was pleased that the lectures and demonstrations I did were very well received. However, one particular question kept popping up: it was about the fact that I was only in my twenties at the time. People seemed really surprised that I was an accomplished medium at such a young age.

I think this was partly because, at that time, the more mature mediums, such as Doris Stokes, Doris Collins and Gordon Higginson, were all frequently appearing in public. This perhaps gave people the idea that a medium must be older to be good.

My response was that you are either a medium or you are not. If you have the qualities that the spirit people think right, they will place you where they want you.

Having said that, maturity, is of course very important in mediumship, as is sensitivity and empathy. However, these things don't necessarily come with age. More often than not, they come with experience, and I certainly felt that I had experienced enough close contact with death to give me at least some of the right qualities for a medium.

And it would seem that the spirit world agreed with me, for my work was soon to be taken to yet another level.

CHAPTER 11
Tracy: The circle of life

I didn't very often receive private telephone calls at work, but when I did, it usually meant something was wrong. My supervisor had just called me out of my tea-break and told me my mum was on the phone, so I immediately rushed back to my office to take the call.

'Hi, Mum, what's up?' I asked.

'It's your dad,' she told me. 'He's got to go into hospital. He needs a heart valve replacement, or he'll die!'

I did my best to calm Mum down, as she was really distraught. She asked me if I would take some time off work to accompany her and Dad to the hospital and she told me we would be allowed to stay there overnight whilst Dad was in the operating theatre. I immediately agreed, and the preparations were made.

When we arrived, we were all made very welcome by the staff, and Dad got ready for the operation he was to have later on that evening. He was in excellent spirits, and just wanted to get it all over and done with so that he could get on with his life again. We stayed until he was taken on a trolley to theatre, where he would remain for many hours, whilst his new heart valve was fitted. He was due back in the ward at around 5 the next morning.

Mum and I were led to our guest room for the night – a Portacabin in the hospital grounds. We chatted for a couple of hours, before settling down at around midnight. No sooner had we turned the light off than the telephone rang. Mum rushed to answer it, immediately assuming there was a problem with Dad. All she could hear was a muffled hissing noise. She put the receiver down, and turned the light off.

For the next couple of hours, however, we couldn't sleep at all, as the telephone kept ringing every few minutes. Sometimes I answered it, sometimes Mum did. A couple of times, when I answered the phone, I thought I could hear a muffled voice saying my name over and over, and later Mum confided that when she answered it, she had also thought she heard a muffled voice calling her name. The whole experience was infuriating, but also extremely spooky, and eventually at 4.30 a.m. we decided to return to the ward to wait for Dad.

As we walked together down the long corridor, there was a bit of a commotion. A man was being wheeled in our direction, surrounded by doctors and nurses. We moved to one side to allow them to pass, and couldn't believe our eyes when we realised that it was Dad lying there on the trolley in front of us. We followed the procession back to the ward, but were asked to wait outside until they had made him comfortable.

When we were eventually allowed to go in, I was shocked to see an angry red line running the whole length of his chest, from just beneath his chin, to underneath his ribcage.

It was a scary sight, and both Mum and I were overcome with relief that he'd made it through the operation. We were told we could sit with him for a while, so we sat one on either side, holding his hand, touching his arm, when suddenly the heart monitor and other equipment began to make a high-pitched bleeping sound, and within seconds doctors and nurses were running in from all directions. We were ushered out of the room and about 20 minutes went by before a doctor came out to explain that Dad's heart had temporarily stopped beating, but that all was well now. We were allowed back into the ward very briefly, and then advised to go home and rest.

During the journey, we recalled the weird telephone calls, and the strange coincidence whereby we had arrived back at the ward at exactly the same time as Dad. We concluded that somehow the spirit world was trying to communicate to us that Dad might be in danger, but that he would receive their help to pull through.

He went on to make an excellent recovery from his operation and it was great to see him sitting up in bed, laughing and joking with us. It was even better the first time he walked us to the end of the ward to wave goodbye. Before long, we were going to pick him up from hospital to bring him home, and we made a special fuss of him as we settled him into the car to begin the journey.

Praying for a miracle

The first couple of weeks at home, Dad seemed to make good progress, but then he suddenly started to deteriorate. He began to suffer from extremely bad headaches, and after a few days he started vomiting. At first Mum thought he was suffering from migraines, but I urged her to get the doctor as I didn't like the sound of his symptoms. The doctor came, but assured Mum that everything was fine, and told her not to worry.

I remember calling round to visit Dad to wish him a happy birthday and take him his present. Mum told me to go straight upstairs to their bedroom, where he had been for the last three weeks. I was shocked at what I saw. Dad was sound asleep, and there was a bowl at the side of the bed full of vomit. He was extremely pale. I shook his arm to wake him, but he did not fully respond. He seemed aware that someone was with him, but he didn't recognise me, and he couldn't be bothered to acknowledge his birthday present. A chill of fear ran through me, and I knew there was something drastically wrong.

I went downstairs and urged Mum to get the doctor. I left the house feeling exceptionally worried, and sent an immediate thought out to the spirit people to help my dad. That night in bed, I meditated, and imagined Sister Josephine passing her wonderful healing energy into his depleted body. I must have drifted off to sleep, but I recall waking up, with a vision of Nana Jackson walking towards me and holding out her hand; she touched me on the side of my face and said three words before disappearing into thin air. The sound of her voice echoed through my mind, as I heard her saying over and over again: 'Help my son.'

Needless to say, I didn't get much sleep for the rest of the night. Somehow I was convinced that my dad had suffered a blood clot to his brain. I'm not sure how or why I thought this; something just seemed to tell me that this was what was wrong with him. The next morning, I rang Mum to see how he was, and to tell her about my experience of the night before. She said that Dad had been very poorly in the night, and that she was really concerned. I told her I was going to ring the doctor myself.

I rang the emergency out-of-hours number, and explained about Dad's operation, and how unwell he had been since coming home from hospital, and I also blurted out that I had a feeling he had a blood clot on his brain. The doctor quite rightly remonstrated with me for diagnosing the problem myself, and advised that he should be the judge of what was wrong with Dad, but he did agree to come out and see him straightaway. Twenty minutes later the GP rang to tell me that he was admitting Dad to hospital for tests and a brain scan and said that I could accompany Mum in the ambulance. I rushed to my parents' house and arrived just as they were putting Dad in the ambulance.

Later that day, we were told that Dad was being transferred to Sheffield's Royal Hallamshire Hospital, where he would be admitted to the Specialist Brain Unit. We were shocked at this news. The doctor went on to explain that the new heart valve had caused problems with Dad's circulation, and as a result he suffered three cerebral haemorrhages (blood clots in his brain). His condition was extremely serious, and had deteriorated rapidly, to the extent that he was now in a deep coma.

The next few weeks were possibly the most stressful I have ever experienced, as my brothers Adrian and Nigel, my sister Lisa, and Mum and I kept a permanent vigil at Dad's bedside. On top of this, I also had to contend with the fact that my husband had just been made redundant, and was frantically searching for a new job, so he was only able to come to the hospital on odd occasions.

Dad was virtually slipping away before our eyes, as he remained in a deep coma, week after week. Eventually static pneumonia set in. Christmas came, and we spent Christmas Day afternoon playing Scrabble next to his bed. A few days later, his breathing became extremely laboured, and he was given a tracheotomy. The operation was successful, but still Dad's condition deteriorated. After he had been lying in a coma for six weeks, the doctors eventually asked Mum to consider, along with the rest of the family, whether or not treatment could be stopped, and my dad be allowed to die. We had an agonising discussion over what was to be done.

Again, I turned my thoughts to the spirit world, and asked for help and guidance. I meditated, and I recall a journey with my Native American Guide, Silver Hawk, who has worked with me from the beginning.

I asked if he could tell me about my dad. All he would say was, 'It will all be sorted out on Thursday'. It was Sunday at that point, and I automatically assumed therefore that it would be Thursday of that week, which would be New Year's Eve; that Dad's treatment would stop, and that he would pass to the spirit world.

I prayed for him each day that week, and couldn't sleep at all on Wednesday night. I felt really ill as we began the journey to Sheffield on Thursday morning. We walked into the ward as usual, and sat down next to him. We had been there only a few minutes, and really couldn't believe our eyes when, for the first time in nearly seven weeks, he looked directly at us and said, quite simply, 'Hello.'

A nurse was passing at that exact moment, and she was as shocked as we were. She walked over to him, and said, 'Hello, Tony, can you hear me OK?' He looked puzzled before responding: 'Yes, nurse, of course I can hear you – but where am I?'

The doctors were called, and after much discussion it was agreed that Dad had made a miraculous recovery. It was totally unexpected, and they had all been under the impression that he had no chance of ever regaining consciousness. It was going to be a Happy New Year, after all!

Reaching rock bottom

Dad went from strength to strength, and was eventually allowed home. Shortly after his return, we discovered that one of the side effects of his illness was epilepsy, for which he would need treatment indefinitely. Unfortunately, as with many people who suffer any kind of brain injury, his personality was also affected. As he recovered, he suffered terrible mood swings and outbursts of anger and frustration at no longer being able to work. These were mostly directed towards my mum, and this eventually led to the breakdown of their marriage a couple of years later.

During this time, my own health had begun to suffer, and all the things that had happened to me took their toll. I had suffered the loss of two babies and two grandparents, and had nearly died myself when my car caught fire. I had lived for two years in a house that had brought me nothing but trouble and sleepless nights, and had had a brief, but intense encounter with Spiritualism. I had worked in a stressful and demanding job, which had in all honesty become too much for me. My marriage was deteriorating rapidly, as my husband and I had grown further and further apart, and I no longer felt he gave me any support.

I was eventually retired from the Civil Service on the grounds of ill health. This was the last straw; total collapse followed. I felt that my world had caved in, and believed there was nothing worth living for any more. I couldn't face a life without a purpose, and quite literally wanted to curl up and die.

During my illness I became restless and, much to my husband's annoyance, wanted to move house again. Luckily, our semi attracted a lot of interest and sold within the first week, so we were able to put in an offer on a three-storey house, which I loved. Thankfully, everything went through smoothly.

Dad came round regularly to help me decorate. I am certain that doing up the house helped him with his recovery, just as much as it helped me with mine. He did a brilliant job and, when the house was finished, I was really proud of all our hard work.

Looking back, I know that I had to go to that house for a purpose, and I am sure that the spirit people engineered our move there in order to start a sequence of events over which I seemingly had no power.

When we first moved there, I felt I was a lost cause, that I had no worth, and no reason to continue living, but when I left that house two years later, I was a confident, outgoing person, and I was just beginning to establish myself as a working medium!

Unexpected help

After the work on the house was completed, I began to consider exactly what my purpose in life now was. I made the occasional visit to Mum's church but I didn't go regularly. However, these visits did help me to begin to think in a spiritual way again. I knew, deep inside, that I wanted to do something with my life that not only made me feel good about myself, but was also useful and helpful to other people.

After my mum and dad broke up, I had done all I could to support each of them as individuals, but they still had their own problems, and from time to time they would call upon me for help. I always offered special help and support to my dad, who now lived alone, but who I felt to be vulnerable due to his ongoing health problems. If I had expected to be helping anyone at that time, it would have been him. However, this was not to be the case. Instead, I was called upon by my mum to help out with my younger brother Nigel, who lived only a few doors away from me in his own flat.

Nigel had suffered from schizophrenia since the age of 16. On good days, he was the most kind, caring and joyous person to be with, but on bad days, he sank to the depths of despair, and there was a darkness about him. This caused him to act irrationally, being destructive to himself and those closest to him.

Nigel was an exceptionally clever young man, with an innate understanding of computers, and he had briefly held down a job as a computer programmer designing games for children. He was also a gifted musician, and spent a fortune on electric keyboards and synthesisers on which he wrote his tunes. He took music lessons, and studied jazz, and was so well-loved by the local community that everyone took his illness for granted, and sometimes forgot how he suffered inside.

Nigel's illness meant that he couldn't always manage some of the most basic day-to-day tasks for himself. He would forget to wash and bathe, didn't bother to tidy his flat, and wasn't able to shop for food or cook a meal. It had therefore been agreed with Social Services and his psychiatrist that Mum would be Nigel's main carer, and that she would provide facilities for him, such as regular hot meals and clean clothes. She also made sure he took his medication on a regular basis.

One day, however, Mum rang me in quite a state, saying that she had come to the end of her tether. She had just started a new relationship with a very nice man, who was really good to her, but Nigel was finding it difficult to accept the situation, so she asked me to help out by giving him the odd meal and keeping an eye on him.

I immediately agreed and Nigel started coming round to me for meals three days per week. My husband wasn't too happy about this when he heard the news, but as he wasn't very often at home when Nigel came around I persevered with my plans. My son Luke was only small at the time, and Nigel always made a huge fuss of him, laughing and joking, and throwing him up in the air, causing fits of giggles all round. My daughter Gemma was just discovering pop music, and would discuss all the latest hits with her Uncle Nigel when he came round.

After tea, Nigel and I would sit and chat, and during those times he would often bring up the subject of Spiritualism. He loved to talk about his good friends Chris and Matt, who ran a healing circle, which he had been attending for several years. Nigel felt that going to this group helped him with his illness, and he enjoyed the company of friends, where he was made to feel welcome and part of something special.

Nigel knew about my breakdown, and tried to encourage me to go with him to the circle to receive healing, and to meet his friends. In fact, he seemed determined that I should attend, and every time he came round, he brought up the subject of me joining the circle and just wouldn't take no for an answer. When I look back now, I realise that he did me a huge favour by introducing me to his healing group. In fact, the whole episode was to be instrumental in helping me achieve the success I now have.

The right time to start

The healing circle met on a Tuesday evening, and the only person I knew there was Nigel. Not surprisingly, I was apprehensive about going along, but I decided to give it a try, as I felt it would help to improve my confidence. I really did want the opportunity to receive some healing to help me feel better. On my first visit, I arrived early and was introduced to Nigel's good friends Chris and Matt. Also present were my sister's mother-in-law Linda, mum's gardener Patrick, and a lovely disabled lady called Joyce. (I later learned that Joyce had known Paul quite well and that she used to sit in a circle with him and Annie Gloster – just one of a multitude of coincidences throughout our lives.)

When everyone was present, we sat in a circle, closed our eyes and relaxed in the peaceful atmosphere that had been created. After a while, Matt stood up, and moved from person to person. He stood behind each one of us and placed his hands upon the area of the body that he felt inspired to touch and to heal. Matt is an exceptional healer, and within moments of him placing his hands at the back of my neck, and later at the top of my head, I felt calmer and more peaceful, as though all my troubles had drifted away.

Chris then talked us through the meditation. I was instantly aware of Silver Hawk drawing close to me, and also my lovely Sister Josephine. Together they told me that the time was now right to begin my work for the spirit world, and that circumstances around me were changing to enable me to do the important work for which I had been chosen. They proceeded to give me pertinent information for each member of the circle, which I was told to relay at the end of the meditation. Everyone seemed both touched and shocked when I passed these messages on.

At the end of the session, Matt turned to the circle and said: 'You've just witnessed a true medium,' after which he turned to me and said, 'You'll go far... but it won't be easy for you.'

I got chatting to Chris afterwards, and there was an affinity between us that I have only known with one or two other people. We knew instantly that we would be good friends, and we swapped telephone numbers and agreed to speak to each other before the circle the next week.

True to her word, Chris telephoned me the very next morning. She told me how impressed she had been with my mediumship the previous night, and said she would do everything she could to help me become established as a working medium, if that was what I wanted. I told her that I wasn't at all sure if mediumship was what I wanted to do. She seemed to understand how I felt, and encouraged me to keep coming along to the circle to build up my confidence, and to practise my work in a safe and friendly environment.

Nigel and I chatted about the circle when he came round for tea. This was something special which he and I shared, and which brought us closer than we had been since our childhood years. He also seemed impressed by my ability as a medium, and constantly encouraged me to do more with my gift.

Chris and I would talk for hours on the telephone about Spiritualism and the spirit world. She always said that I was a natural medium, as I seemed to know instinctively how things should be done.

I often expressed to her at that time how lonely I felt and in need of teaching myself, and how I yearned for someone to come along who could enable me to feel confident enough to work as a medium myself. She always told me that I would never meet anyone who could teach me more than I already knew, which I thought was a really strange thing for her to say, and I didn't really believe it. Strangely enough, Paul has said exactly the same thing to me many times in the six years I have known and worked with him.

A circle of my own

After I had been going to the circle for a few months, Chris rang me up one morning with a proposition. She was looking for someone to run a development circle for novice mediums at my mum's church, and wondered if I would be interested.

Initially I refused because I really didn't feel up to the job but eventually agreed – after a great deal of persuasion.

The group began with about 15 people and, once word got out about the plans I had, there was a waiting list of others wanting to join. However, I stuck with the original 15 members, as I felt this was a manageable number.

Some weeks were spent just meditating, and feeding back our experiences. I found it incredibly easy to link with each member of the circle and translate what their meditation meant to them as individuals. I also gave little snippets of messages as I worked my way around the sitters, once the meditations had ended.

I encouraged the group to practise their psychic abilities, and we used crystals, ribbons, paper and other psychic tools to give messages to each other. Another thing I got them to do was to prepare presentations on Spiritualist philosophy, as I knew that they would be required to talk about the principles of Spiritualism, should they ever be privileged enough to go on and work as mediums in Spiritualist churches.

An extraordinary demonstration

One of the most astounding things I recall arranging was a trance demonstration by a well-known local medium called Les Driver.

Trance is a form of mediumship that allows a more direct type of communication to occur. This is because the spirit communicators have a greater degree of control and can influence the medium's mind more easily. When the medium enters the state of trance, the spirit communicators are able to use and manipulate the voice and mannerisms of the medium, to give the impression they are *inside* their body. This is, however, *not* the case. The spirit is merely operating from within the medium's aura, and is able to communicate in a more direct manner, without the need for the medium to relay the information for them.

Les arrived punctually, and advised the circle not to be shocked by anything they were about to witness, but to sit back and relax, and enjoy the opportunity to spend some quality time in direct communication with the spirit world. The group was encouraged to ask questions of the spirit communicators, and to participate fully in the demonstration.

He soon entered the trance state, and a wise and wonderful guide began to communicate. He spoke to us of spirituality and Spiritualism, with great knowledge and love. He invited us to ask questions, and I was proud of everyone. They made intelligent and pertinent enquiries about the spirit world. Then, quite suddenly, the guide pointed to me and began to speak.

'Child, you must stop your doubting,' he said. 'You are destined to work as a medium, and the pages have already been written, so it is time for you to turn them over and allow the story to unfold. You will travel North, South, East and West in this country, and you will travel overseas to do the work of the spirit world, and when you return, you will open your own sanctuary of love and light. Accept your destiny, child, and lead the way instead of asking us to light the way for you.'

With this, the guide slowly faded away, and everyone looked shocked at what had been said.

Soon, another guide was speaking to us. This time it was a vicar, who preached his Christian beliefs and then followed his sermon by singing very loudly in the most amazing voice. He sang the hymn 'Jerusalem' in beautiful clear notes that filled the room, and everyone was amazed at what they were witnessing. About halfway through the song, the room was filled with the singing of a choir, which resonated and grew louder until it reached a crescendo of magnificent and ear-splitting sound. Then, quite suddenly, it stopped, as the next guide moved forward to speak.

We were all stunned by what we had witnessed. I, for one, had never experienced anything like that before – it was absolutely amazing, and I felt privileged to have been present. However, some members of the circle had been quite unnerved by what they had seen and heard, and the new guide immediately acknowledged this, and proceeded to settle the group down by passing on messages to them all.

None of us wanted that evening to come to an end, and it is an experience that remains vivid in my memory today. When I spoke to Les after he had recovered from his demonstration, I told him what had happened. He was very modest, saying that none of it was down to him, it was down to the spirit world – and this point has always stuck in my mind. For it is never the medium who should be praised, but the spirit people who choose to communicate through that medium.

Taking the next step

I continued to teach my development circle, but as the weeks passed, I began to feel slightly perturbed. Some members of the circle showed great promise and I sincerely believed that at least two of them had the potential to progress further. But how could I introduce them to working in Spiritualist churches when I wasn't a working medium myself? Surely the booking secretaries at the churches wouldn't accept my recommendation when they had no knowledge of me or my work?

I kept trying to think of ways around this problem. But in the end, I could see no other option than to accept some bookings myself, with a view to giving my students the opportunity to work alongside me on the odd occasion.

It was a scary thought, but I came to the conclusion that I had to feel the fear – and do it anyway.

CHAPTER 12
Paul: Mediums and the media

As my reputation as a medium grew, I started to travel more and meet a lot of interesting people. I was also delighted to receive opportunities to talk about my work in the media. I had already started working on the radio, but it seemed that the spirit world felt I was now ready to appear on television as well. I never questioned the spirit people or their motives, but just did my best to share my knowledge with as many people as possible, wherever I was directed to go.

Somehow people came into my life at just the right moment to help me progress. One person I was introduced to was a lady called Barbara Kelly, who, together with her husband Bernard Braden, ran a business supplying after-dinner speakers, TV and radio personalities and interesting individuals to television, radio and theatrical companies. They were, some years before my time, famous television personalities themselves. Barbara used to be on a programme called *What's my Line?* and Bernard hosted a consumer programme known as *Braden's Week*.

My first television appearance

Barbara had said that she would be in touch if anything suitable for me turned up. Quite soon after, a TV company were making a pilot programme on the paranormal, and they contacted her to see if she knew of any reputable mediums.

She kindly gave them my name. They had unsuccessfully tried to contact me whilst I was away in Scotland and so she gave me their telephone number and suggested I call them straightaway.

As it turned out, the producer wanted me to go to London the following day. I was slightly overawed at the prospect of demonstrating my work on television. Nevertheless, the next day, I set off for London in good time, and arrived at the Wyvern Rogers Television Company, just opposite the Duke of York Theatre, well in advance of my appointment time. I waited in the reception area, and was eventually greeted by a very jolly chap, who came over, smiling and chatting as he put out his hand.

'Hello,' he said, 'you must be Paul Norton.' We shook hands.

'Yes,' I replied. He introduced himself. 'I'm Brian Izzard, the producer. We're just waiting for the others to arrive, and then we'll be ready to begin,' he said, cheerfully.

A stream of people walked into reception, and straight into a nearby office.

After a while, Brian stood in the doorway of the office, and shouted over enthusiastically, 'Paul, come on in and meet the others.'

Brian introduced me to everyone. 'This is the Reverend Graham St John Willey, Peter and Mary Harrison, Aelwyn Roberts, John Clive…' I smiled and said hello. Almost immediately each one of them started firing questions at me, as if all trying to compete with each other, everybody was talking at once.

'What do you think about ouija boards?'

'You must be communicating with the Devil.'

'Isn't what you do mind-reading?'

'How do you feel about these comments?'

I paused for a few seconds to gather my thoughts and answered each question in turn, after which even more questions were fired at me. By the time I had finished, my head was spinning.

'Paul,' said Brian, now even more enthusiastically, 'you have just acquitted yourself marvellously. You're perfect, just what we're looking for.'

He went on to explain that they had wanted to see my reaction to pressure and of course hear my views and my answers to the questions I had been posed.

As he stood up to shake my hand, and lead me to the door, Brian told me he would be in touch soon. I didn't hear anything for a few weeks, and then quite unexpectedly I received a letter from Wyvern Rogers inviting me to appear on the programme. It was going to be called *David Frost's Night Visitors,* and was due to be filmed at Cardiff Castle. The letter gave further details of times, travel and accommodation arrangements.

After I arrived at the Castle, I was immediately shown to my dressing room. They'd arranged for everyone to wear evening clothes, because the programme was being filmed as an after-dinner discussion. I was kitted out with a bow tie, dinner jacket and trousers.

Then I was handed over to the make-up team. One of the other 'dinner guests' was already there being made up; she turned towards me, smiled and said hello. I recognised her as Siân Phillips, the actress.

Afterwards I was taken to along to meet the others. By this time, Peter and Mary Harrison had arrived, along with Graham Willey, Frances Ommaney (a television producer), Peter Ramster (an Australian psychologist), Aelwyn Roberts and the singer Lynsey de Paul.

We all started chatting and getting to know each other, and, as we did so, David Frost came into the room and shook each of our hands whilst having a few words individually with us about the filming. I was just getting into the swing of things when a striking young lady entered, and introduced herself.

'Hello, I'm Toyah,' she said.

Toyah Willcox was the final guest to appear on the programme.

The television company had arranged a meal for us all, which was very much appreciated after the long journey. I sat between Lynsey and Toyah, and they were both very friendly indeed. Lynsey chatted about her house in Highgate, London, and the resident ghost they had and how she was hoping to move. She told me she was friends with Doris Collins and that Doris had helped her a great deal.

I told Lynsey how I had become involved in mediumship and how Doris had both impressed and inspired me all those years ago, when I had first seen her work as a medium. I agreed with Lynsey that Doris had been a great help to many people, and asked her to pass on my good wishes.

The programme was being filmed in three different sections. There was a part on out-of-body experiences, another on reincarnation and the last section on Spiritualism. In between each one, Siân Phillips would read a story about a spirit or a ghost, or something along those lines. I watched each part being filmed and found it all very interesting, listening to the stories each person had to tell, followed by the experts' opinions and explanations. However, after five hours of retakes it got a bit monotonous, and I was just praying that the part I was in would go smoothly, as it was getting late by this time.

It wasn't until 9.30 p.m. that they finally got round to the section on Spiritualism. I was led onto the set, where some chairs and a sofa had been neatly arranged by the fireplace in the Great Hall. I was placed next to Toyah. Graham Willey was sitting next to me on a stool, Frances Ommaney was opposite with David Frost, and Mary Harrison beside the fireplace.

Before the filming commenced I was briefly shown a list of questions that David had to choose from. I had no idea which ones he was going to ask me, so I sent out a thought to the spirit world in the hope that the spirits would give me some guidance.

'Are you ready? Three, two, one and action!' The camera started rolling. David first asked me to describe my work as a medium. He then made a few suggestions as to the kinds of people who would come along to see me and the types of messages they would receive, at which point he moved on to question Toyah. She said that she fully believed in my abilities but she raised doubts as to whether or not people should contact their dead loved ones through mediums and Spiritualism.

At this point Graham Willey joined in, and stated that the Bible described these spirit people as nothing but demonic angels.

I pointed out that spirit people provided astounding evidence about themselves and their loved ones, and they almost always poured out their love to their people.

'How can this possibly be demonic?' I asked. 'I can see these people in the spirit world and they look and act only slightly differently from people who are alive.' Before Graham had the chance to respond, David interrupted with more questions.

The filming went on without a hitch, so there was no retake for us.

Some months later, I received a copy of *Night Visitors*. It had already been shown on TV but I had missed it. The finished version was really impressive, and I am happy to say they only cut out a little bit of what I had said and gave me a very fair hearing.

This isn't always the case. Often when mediums have appeared on television in the past, the presenters have tended to try and make fools of them, or important aspects of the interview have been edited out before the programme is shown on TV. In my case, this wasn't so, and I was very pleased about it.

Being on the front line

Whenever an opportunity like *Night Visitors* comes along, or the chance to speak to a reporter, I generally take it, because it gives me a chance to bring something into the lives of people who perhaps wouldn't normally come into contact with the spirit world and share my gifts. However, it still comes as a bit of a shock when I see articles and stories printed about my work in the newspapers.

One Sunday afternoon, I was taking a few minutes to read the papers and catch up on what was happening in the world. As I opened one of the magazines I saw a photograph of a woman I knew. Above the picture the headline read: 'When The Medium Contacted My Fiancé I Was A Bag Of Nerves.' This was an article printed in the *Sunday Mirror* magazine about a private sitting I'd given to a lady at Mansfield, Nottinghamshire.

About three months after the *Night Visitors* project, I received a telephone call from Barbara Kelly, who told me that a researcher from the *Kilroy* programme wanted me to appear on their forthcoming show about the paranormal. I was quite happy to oblige. They asked me if there was anyone who had had a sitting or message from me who would consider going along to support the discussion.

Only a few weeks before, I had gone to Mansfield to do a sitting for a lady called Margaret Jones. When I first met her, I could see that she was desperate and so I gave her my telephone number so that she could call me and arrange a private meeting, which she did.

The sitting had gone very well indeed, and the person who Margaret had wanted to hear from had come through, loud and clear. As it transpired, Margaret had lost her fiancé, Kevin. Apparently he'd been burning some rubbish in the back garden, there was a sudden gust of wind and the flames caught his clothes, resulting in him catching fire and suffering severe burns. He had gone to hospital but had passed away a few days later. Despite my own sad losses, I couldn't even begin to imagine how this poor woman felt; I just knew I had to give her some sort of comfort, something to help keep her going.

I immediately thought of Margaret for the *Kilroy* show, and when I phoned her she readily agreed to provide, as the researchers had asked, a testimony of the sitting for the programme.

Margaret was asked to take along her son Richard. Apparently, he didn't believe in mediums. He thought that either Margaret had given me clues, or I'd somehow got the information from her, and the researchers for the show thought this would be a good angle from which to approach the subject.

I was picked up at the station by one of the drivers and taken straight to the TV studios. Margaret and Richard were already in the green room with a host of other people. The programme normally went out live, but this one was to be recorded for the following day. It was soon time to start filming and we were all asked to take our seats in the studio.

Because I was one of the 'invited experts', I was placed on the front row. Susan Blackmore, the well-known psychologist and sceptic, was sitting next to me, and next to her was Barbara Smoker from the Secular Society, then Doris Collins. Nella Jones, the psychic detective, and Ian Wilson, the author were sitting behind.

The programme started with various suggestions about the paranormal and Spiritualism, and then people were given the opportunity to voice their opinions in turn. Barbara Smoker soon tackled Doris Collins and then took a pot shot at the medium Stephen O'Brien, who wasn't even present to defend himself. She just wouldn't accept any of the explanations given; she seemed not to have any beliefs in anything. Doris responded well, and gave a good account of how mediumship really worked. Nella Jones also managed to put across her point in a polite and effective manner.

Author Ian Wilson began by tearing mediums apart, in particular Doris Stokes.

This was the point when I became involved. I told Ian that nobody had ever disproved Doris Stokes' work and added that it would have been more appropriate for him to have called her a fraud whilst she was alive and then she would have been able to defend herself.

Susan Blackmore interrupted and said that mediums 'cold read' audiences. In other words, she was saying they fish around for information and make generalised statements.

'So, would you call a name and address and important personal information generalised?' I countered. She never directly responded and continued to call it cold reading. I wish I had thought to ask her to demonstrate what she actually meant. It would have been very good for Susan to give a demonstration of 'cold reading' the audience. Then one of the mediums could have given a demonstration of mediumship. That way, people would have been able to see the differences, and might have formed their own judgements.

Kilroy moved on to Margaret and Richard, who were sitting behind me. Margaret gave a very clear account of what had happened during her sitting. It was so moving to listen to her story of tragedy overcome by hope, and by the time she'd finished speaking everyone was quite emotional. Richard added that he thought it was all nonsense, even though he admitted that his mother appeared better in herself since receiving her message from Kevin.

After the show

Once the filming was done, we were all ushered into the green room, where they'd put on a marvellous spread. A gentleman I recognised approached me.

'Hello, Paul,' he said. 'I'm Laurie O'Leary.'

Laurie O'Leary had been the famed manager of Doris Stokes.

We had a very long chat indeed, during which he told me many wonderful stories about Doris.

'Come over, and I'll introduce you to Doris Collins,' he said. I followed him over to where Doris was sitting. Since Doris Stokes' passing, Laurie had started working with Doris Collins to continue the work of promoting mediumship.

I told Doris that she had been the first medium I had ever seen, and said how much her own work had inspired me to go forward and help people. Doris was pleased and said that she always hoped her work would encourage younger mediums. After the *Kilroy* show, Doris and I became quite friendly and would often speak on the telephone. She very kindly agreed to write the foreword to a book that I wrote in 1995. Here is what she wrote:

It is vitally important that younger mediums are prepared to take over from us older ones and I have spent many years working towards this end.

I am absolutely delighted that there are dedicated sensitives like Paul Norton who are ready to carry on helping those in need.

Having seen him work, I am quite sure that he will be one of the very best of the young mediums.

This book will serve as an introduction to a brilliant young man and I would like to take this opportunity to wish Paul every success and a long and happy life for the future.

Doris Collins
Willen Village, 1995

Laurie was a charming and interesting man to talk to. He and I also agreed to keep in touch, and he gave me his new telephone number. Over the years, we have had many conversations about both Doris Stokes and Doris Collins. Even though I do the work myself, I will never cease to be amazed at their sheer determination to spread the word about the spirit world; their achievements have always given me inspiration and hope.

I said a quick hello to Nella Jones, who was deep in conversation with a small group of people, and then went over to have a chat with Margaret and Richard. Kilroy thanked me for being on the show and he seemed very impressed with the way I had handled the remarks from the sceptics.

In fact, he had been so touched by Margaret's story that he'd decided to write an article about it in his weekly column in the *Sunday Mirror Magazine*. The article was divided into two parts: the first part was Margaret's story, and the second was Richard's.

This is what Kilroy wrote:

Margaret's Story

When Margaret Jones's fiancé Kevin died on May 24th 1991, at the age of 34, the 45-year-old Nottingham woman was determined to get in touch with him.

I needed to know that he was still around, she said. I'd seen the medium Paul Norton at the Arts and Leisure Centre in Mansfield and I'd asked if he'd do a private sitting. He came to my house in October last year.

Before he arrived, I said, 'Kevin, the one thing that will really convince me that you're still there is if Paul knows you changed your name. That's all the proof that I need.'

The first thing Paul said was, 'Who's David?' I felt like a bag of nerves – that was Kevin's real name. I knew he was in contact with Kevin.

There were so many things that Kevin told Paul that only Kevin knew. Paul told me that the shower kept blowing up, and it did. He said that all the clocks in the house had stopped, and they had. He said that Kevin was covered in tattoos – he was. He told me that he used to bite his nails until they bled, and he did.

There were lots of things that no one else could have possibly known. For instance, Kevin told Paul that a week after he died I had given his new shoes to my brother, Eddie. But before I'd put them in the car, I'd sniffed them to make sure they smelled all right. Nobody could know that.

Through Paul, Kevin has helped me. I was thinking of moving to be near my son, Michael, in Chelmsford. During my session with Paul, he asked, 'Why are you thinking of moving to Chelmsford?' Then he told me the very personal reason that I had for thinking of moving, and said, 'Kevin says you are not to go. It's the worst thing you could possibly do. It will all sort itself out soon.' I did as I was told and it has all been resolved, even though I never believed it could be.

I know that Kevin is still here. My bedroom is like a sauna. It's been like that ever since he passed away. I have to have my windows open all the time – it's so hot. It's his presence. It's not just me that feels it. As soon as you get to the door you can feel the heat. The bedroom was his favourite room. We decorated it together.

My 23-year-old son, Richard, says that Paul could have gleaned the information from anywhere. That annoys me. It causes trouble between us. He keeps telling me that Paul's a con-man. I get so irate I could hit him – I could really hit him.

He winds me up a lot. I usually tolerate him because he's my son. If it was anyone else, I'd tell him to clear off.

Richard's Story

It seemed to me pretty daft. I just thought that she was clutching at straws. I thought there was a logical explanation for everything that Paul told her. He could have picked up things in conversation or made deductions. There are a lot of things related to Kevin in my mum's house. It can't be difficult for someone to pick up bits and pieces of information. They don't come from the dead.

I didn't know how he could have known about the shoes and I have to admit that her bedroom is always hot. I don't know why. It's not that hot anywhere else in the house but it is hot in my mum's bedroom. I can't remember if it was always like that.

She used to get on my nerves with what Paul told her. It would be, 'Paul said this, Paul said that.' I just used to turn off and not listen to her. I had an explanation for everything she'd been told, but she wouldn't listen to me.

I tried to keep quiet because it was obviously giving her comfort. But I wished she would pack it in. I was worried that she would get hurt by finding out that someone was making things up and lying to her. I didn't trust Paul Norton and I didn't want her to end up feeling disillusioned and upset. She'd have been shattered. I was also worried that she would be made to look like a fool. She'd told all her friends what he'd said. She told them how convinced she was that he was communicating with Kevin, and that Kevin was still around. If Paul was proved to be a fake she would lose face and be humiliated.

What Paul told her did comfort her. It gave her a lot of hope and she felt secure that Kevin had not gone off and left her on her own. That's why I didn't come straight out and say that it was all rubbish. I just tried to imply that it could all go wrong. I was only trying to prepare her.

Paul used to argue with me constantly. I told him it was all nonsense. I said there was only one way that I could be convinced that he was genuine, and the day he came up with it, I'd change my mind.

It was something that only I knew. When Kevin was in the Chapel of Rest and we went to pay our last respects we went in one at a time. When I went in, I put my hand in the coffin and stroked the side of his face. I didn't tell anyone what I'd done and no one saw me do it.

A couple of days later, Paul said that he'd get the proof for me. He said, 'You told me that there was only one thing that would convince you. Kevin knows what it is. He's going to tell me.'

He said, 'Did you put your hand into the coffin and stroke Kevin's face?' I was speechless. I knew nobody else could have known. Now I have a different view, although I still find it hard to believe that we can receive messages from the other side. But I do understand now why Mum is so convinced.

Afterwards, Richard and Margaret also became very good friends. We often spoke on the phone and when I spoke to Margaret, although she was still occasionally feeling low, in general she seemed much stronger and more able to cope with life's obstacles because of the message I had given her from Kevin.

The blessings of mediumship

Through my work as a medium, I have been fortunate enough to travel extensively and meet some wonderful people, including some of the world's finest mediums. I realise that mediumship has given me a great sense of purpose in life. I went from being an unruly teenager to a responsible adult, who not only accepted the job of helping my friend Daz to live independently, but also took on the burden of trying to relieve the grief of the many bereaved people with whom I have come into contact over the years. Mediumship is not an easy career to follow, but, for me, it seems to have been made easier by the fact that I have been guided along the right path – a path that has helped me to progress and take my work to a wider audience.

In reality, my relationship with the media has always been a good one. I am pleased to see that the paranormal and mediumship have recently become more widely accepted in our society, partly through the many magazines, newspapers and television shows that have emerged in order to meet the needs of the many people who now want to find out more about the afterlife.

However, nothing is more rewarding for me than working with people face to face, either in a theatre or in a one-to-one meeting. I have discovered over the years that radio and television programmes are often heavily edited and so they don't always give a true reflection of the medium's work. This is why working live is a really thrilling experience not only for the medium, but also for those receiving the messages.

CHAPTER 13
Tracy: The turning point

The first person I spoke to about my decision to start taking bookings at spiritualist churches was my good friend Chris Merrick. As the booking secretary for Mum's church, I knew that she would be able to offer me sound advice. She did better than that. Within hours, she had passed my name on to many Spiritualist churches in the area, and within a few days I had my first booking at Edwinstowe for the following Sunday.

Chris accompanied me to the church, and luckily she was also able to act as chairperson for the service. I got through the philosophy explanation painlessly, and found that the congregation were attentive and receptive. Following this, I then launched into the clairvoyance part of the evening, and managed to give about six very convincing messages to different members of the audience. I was quite shocked at the end, when they all started to applaud. Apparently I was a success!

After the service, the booking secretary rushed up with her diary to give me more bookings. I was also approached by two other booking secretaries for churches in Mansfield, who wanted me to work for them too.

I went home feeling elated, and couldn't wait to speak to Chris the next day to find out what she thought. She put me straight on a few things, but nonetheless she was extremely pleased at how well I had done. I will never be able to thank her enough for all the effort she put into helping me to start my career as a medium. Without her behind me at that time, I'm sure I wouldn't be where I am now. She has been a tremendous friend to me.

I was soon inundated with bookings. The phone never seemed to stop ringing, and there was always someone at the door asking for a private reading!

Still troubled by doubts

Despite my popularity as a medium, I still wrestled with my inner self about my ability to do the work. Some of the churches I went to seemed like extremely cold and unreceptive places.

After I had been working regularly for a couple of months, I received a phone call out of the blue, asking if I would be prepared to accept a short-notice booking at the Spiritualist church in Worksop. From what I had heard, this was a beautiful church, and it was looked upon as being a huge feather in your cap if the congregation there liked you.

As it happened, it was not an easy night. I only gave four messages, and I knew by the end of the evening that my work had not gone down too well. When I located Chris in the audience she gave me a look which said, 'Don't be too disheartened.' But I felt terrible and couldn't wait to get away.

Just as Chris and I were leaving, the president of the church approached and what she said left me devastated for days afterwards.

'Young lady,' she said, imperiously, 'I just wanted to let you know that you do show some promise in your work. However, my suggestion to you would be to get yourself back into development for a while – you're not ready for the platform yet.'

I didn't reply – I just walked out of the door. Nothing Chris said to try to console me on the way home could make me feel better. I felt as if I had shown myself up, and that I couldn't possibly honour any of the bookings I had accepted at other churches over the rest of the year. It was July, and I felt there was no way I could possibly continue to work as a medium if that was the opinion of one of the most prestigious churches in the area.

I argued within myself, saying, 'But what about all the other places who think your work is good?' They must be wrong, I thought. All of them are wrong and I'm just fooling myself. I'm never going to make it as a medium, it's just not meant to be.

I decided that I must have a really serious talk with the spirit people, and I told them in no uncertain terms that I wasn't prepared to continue their work, if they were going to put me through ordeals like the one at Worksop. While I accepted that I must learn from these experiences, and that humility was part of the required attitude for mediumship, my confidence couldn't take too many knocks, and so could they please make it a gentler journey for me from now on? So I gave them an ultimatum. I told them I was prepared to do this work for one year only. If, at the end of that time, I was still feeling uncomfortable, then I would not be able to continue. I ended by saying that I wanted to make the President of Worksop Church eat her words, and so within the year they must ask me for another booking.

I think it did me good to get all this off my chest, and to make a firm commitment to myself and to the spirit world to stick with the work for a little bit longer. The first thing I decided to do to get myself on track was to enrol on a couple of courses with the Spiritualists National Union. I passed both with flying colours, and this gave me a great incentive to proceed with my spiritual work.

It was 31 July 2000 when I gave the spirit world their ultimatum. On 31 July 2001, exactly a year to the day after I had made that bargain with the spirits, I was asked to demonstrate once more at Worksop Spiritualist Church. Of course I was nervous before I went along, but it went really well. There were about 100 people in the church that Saturday night, and oh, how it made my heart swell at the end of the service when the clapping seemed to go on for hours and there were cheers from the congregation.

Growing in confidence

During that year, my work and my confidence went from strength to strength, but it wasn't all a bed of roses, for I also had to face a traumatic and tragic loss, which rocked me to the very core of my being.

I did, however, establish myself as a medium. I served at a variety of different Spiritualist churches around the country and my work was always very well received. Word spread and my reputation grew. Many of the people I met were very kind, and did all they could to help me progress. On one occasion I was asked to take a special meeting at Newark.

The third message I gave that night was particularly memorable. I pointed to an attractive young woman and told her that her mother – who had passed with breast cancer – was there. I described how she looked, the type of clothes she wore, her hair, and also mentioned some pieces of jewellery she'd left after she died. I talked about someone being a model – the girl's sister was a model. I told her about some problems she had been having in a relationship, which she confirmed were correct. I also mentioned relevant birthdays and addresses of people within the family; I asked who 'Snow White' was and told the girl this was a private family joke. She confirmed that, yes, 'Snow White' was her mum's nickname for her. As I drew to the end of the message, the girl in the audience was in tears, and as I was about to sit down, she blurted out, 'Can you please tell my mum that I love her?' As I looked around the audience I don't think there was a dry eye in the house. Everyone was crying; it was a beautiful, but sad moment.

Another memorable evening was at Bourne Spiritualist church in Lincolnshire. It took me an hour and a half to get there, only to find the tiniest little church I had ever been in and a congregation of only six people.

I began to work, making a joke that they should all be in for a message tonight. Fortunately, they were a nice bunch of people, very responsive, and not in the least bit perturbed by the fact that only a few of them were there.

At the end of my second message, I could feel the very strong presence of a lady who wanted to communicate with her husband. I knew instinctively that the lady's name was Hilda, and so I asked who knew her.

A very distinguished-looking elderly gentleman, wearing a dinner jacket and bow tie, immediately responded, saying that he knew Hilda and that she had indeed been his wife. I said that she was telling me that when he first set eyes upon her, he had thought she was an angel from up above. He nodded in agreement. I also told of how he used to push her in a wheelchair, and had to deliver care of a very personal nature. I said he was with her when she died, and that he still spoke regularly to her now she was in the spirit world. I described a photograph of her, which he kept in his bedroom, and mentioned a connection with Corby. He confirmed that all of these were correct. At the end of the message the gentleman was in tears, and took out his handkerchief to wipe his face. I thought no more of this, and went on to give two other messages that night.

At the end of the service, the old gentleman approached me and took my hands in his. He was overwhelmed by the message he had received, and he said he wanted to prove to me just how accurate the message had been. He handed me a book – an account of his own life as a psychic artist. He wrote in the front of the book, 'To Tracy, from your new friend in Corby, Tom Hunter'.

I began to read the book when I got home, and was amazed to read in the opening pages, Tom's description of his first meeting with his wife-to-be, Hilda, who he could only describe as an angel! I read on avidly, to discover that everything else in my message to him was documented in his book.

I thought this was amazing proof from the spirit world that I was on the right track.

A tragic loss

In May 2001, I was extremely busy, and it was to be my brother Nigel's thirtieth birthday on 25 May. I called round to see him early that week; he was over at my nan's, and I spent a pleasant half-hour with them both, chatting about the weather and his plans for his birthday. Nigel was in good spirits at that time as he had a new girlfriend, Lynn, and it was good to see him looking well and happy.

Strangely enough, I hadn't bought him a birthday card, as on 24 May I was booked to do private sittings all day at Moorends Spiritualist church. When I got there they told me that they had booked in eight sittings for me. I knew I was going to feel drained at the end of it all, but aimed to do my very best for the people coming to see me. I had a good morning, and the sittings went really well. At lunchtime, there was a buffet, and the other mediums and I gathered for a light lunch before we started on the afternoon's work. We were all ready for a rest, and some of the people who had been present at the church's previous Sunday evening service were having a bit of a giggle about one of the messages the medium had given.

Apparently the medium was trying to describe the conditions in which a gentleman had passed to the spirit world. She had said that she felt pain all over her body, but couldn't quite work out why – to which the recipient of the message had retorted that the source of the pain was a bloody great train running over him! Everyone burst out laughing, me included, but I did think it was slightly irreverent of us to be laughing about the dead in this way.

After a successful day I went home, feeling exhausted, and went straight to bed when I got in. I was just overcome by an overwhelming tiredness, and knew I had to have a bit of a sleep before I started bathing the kids and tackling the huge pile of ironing, which was waiting for me in the kitchen. I never imagined when I nodded off to sleep at around 6 p.m. that I would be awoken about an hour later by my husband, shaking me violently and urging me to get up.

'What's wrong? What's wrong?' I stammered.

'You'd better get round to your mum's,' he said. 'Nigel's thrown himself in front of a train! He's dead.'

My husband never was one for choosing his words carefully. However, his bluntness didn't bother me – I just knew I had to get round to my mum's as soon as possible. As I got ready to go out, I kept telling myself that it wasn't true, that Nigel had tried taking his life before and it hadn't worked. I don't remember getting dressed, or driving the car. I just remember the sound of my mum's sobbing as I walked through the front door. Nigel's girlfriend Lynn and her friend were there; everyone was speaking at once, but no one was making any sense. 'Quiet!' I shouted. 'What's happened?'

Lynn gabbled something about receiving a telephone call from Nigel at about 6 p.m. He had told her he was on the train lines at Welham just outside Retford, and he was about to jump. When she was cut off, she had immediately telephoned the police to inform them of what had happened, in the hope that they could prevent an accident. She had driven up to

Welham with her friend looking for Nigel, but there was no sign of him. She couldn't get hold of him on the phone either, so she went home to wait for news. About an hour later, she received notification from the police that a young man had jumped in front of a train at Welham, but his identity was not yet confirmed. Lynn had come straight round to Mum's to tell her what was happening. At this point Mum was slightly hysterical, so I asked Lynn and her friend to leave.

I immediately rang my husband and asked him to start phoning round. I told him that he should try the transport police, the hospital and the local police in Retford.

He rang back to say pretty much what we already knew – that a young man had jumped in front of a train at Welham, but as yet they were unable to identify the body, which had been taken to the mortuary at Bassetlaw District Hospital. It was around 8.30 when we received this news. People came and went – friends of the family, people who knew Nigel well and who had heard a rumour. My mum just sat quietly crying the whole time.

At 11.30 that night the transport police finally arrived – five and a half hours after the incident. They came to tell my mum that her son, aged 29 years 11 months, had thrown himself in front of a goods train at approximately 6 p.m. that evening.

My mum became angry, shouting and screaming at the policeman. When she had calmed down, he sat on the floor and cried with her. After the police had gone, I rang my other brother Adrian and my sister Lisa, and they both came to the house. I also rang my dad and arranged for a taxi to go and pick him up. The hardest thing I have ever had to do in my whole life was to accompany my mum across the road to where my nan lives, and to wake her up and hear her wails as she learned that her grandson was dead. She was 83 at the time, and kept saying over and over, 'Why didn't they take me? I'm old, it should have been me.'

None of us could understand why this had happened. We all felt we had let Nigel down in some way, and the pain we suffered was beyond description.

Comfort from the spirit world

When I finally got to bed at around 5 a.m. I couldn't sleep. I was worried about my brother, and what had happened to him. I prayed that someone in the spirit world would be there to guide him to a safe place and look after him. I asked for some sign from Nigel that he was OK. I suppose this is what everyone wants to know in these circumstances, and being a medium doesn't make you any different in this respect.

A strange thing happened. Suddenly I was aware of my spirit guide Silver Hawk standing quite clearly in front of me. He told me I was to be allowed to see my brother for one final time to say goodbye, but that this was only because Nigel needed my help. I must urge him to look for my Grandad Wilf, who was waiting for him.

I experienced a feeling of moving forward at a great pace, then stopping very suddenly. It seemed dark all around me and I couldn't see; I only knew that I wanted to move forward again but wasn't allowed to.

Suddenly Nigel was standing in front of me. He spoke to me, saying he could hear people all around him but that he couldn't see anyone. He felt really bad because it was dark. I could see him quite clearly – he was wearing a particular blue T-shirt that he liked, jeans and trainers. I shouted to him urgently, to look for Grandad Wilf. Over and over again I said it, and then suddenly there was a blinding light and Grandad was there; he took Nigel by the hand, and they just faded away. My guide stood in front of me afterwards with a smile on his face. After this I slept, a deep peaceful sleep.

The only person who really believed me when I described this experience was my mum. Why? Because I had described perfectly the clothes Nigel had been wearing.

The funeral took a couple of weeks to organise, as there had to be a post-mortem. However, the people of Retford did Nigel proud and turned out in force to pay their respects to a well-known local character.

Mum hired a marquee for her back garden for the 'wake' and everyone helped prepare sandwiches and nibbles for the hundreds of family members, friends and neighbours who came to say farewell to Nigel. I think it really pleased my mum to know how well thought of he had been. Although it was an upsetting day, it went as smoothly as could be expected on such an occasion. The saddest aspect was that one of the things that had bothered Nigel throughout his life was that he thought no one liked him, and that he wasn't good enough. However, the number of people who turned up to mourn his passing proved him very wrong indeed.

Feeling let down

After the funeral, life got back to normal very quickly, but inside I was fighting a raging battle with the spirit world. For one thing I was exceptionally angry that I hadn't been warned about my brother's death. I couldn't come to terms with the fact that I had spent the day of his suicide giving private sittings at a local Spiritualist church, and at no time had any of the spirits said to me, 'Tracy, your brother needs help – he is contemplating taking his life.'

I couldn't understand it. Surely the spirit world could, and should have let me know what was about to happen? However, I cast my mind back, and remembered a strange incident that had happened at Mum's Spiritualist church the weekend before Nigel's death. I had gone along on the Saturday to watch a local medium, with whom I was very friendly, and was extremely fond of – Ann Anderson. I have a great deal of respect for Ann as a medium, so I was quite shocked that night when she couldn't seem to find anyone to accept her first message. The message was about someone who had been feeling very depressed and who had taken their life by jumping in front of a train. She mentioned a place called Clarborough (about a mile away from Welham, where Nigel died), and there were some other points that I can no longer recall. However, Ann had to leave the message, as no one within the church accepted it.

This incident, together with the harrowing story of someone who had taken their life by jumping in front of a train at Moorends, made me think that the spirit world *had* been trying to warn me, or maybe open my mind to the possibility of someone being killed by a train in preparation for what was to come.

Some years before, around the time that Nigel had first been diagnosed as schizophrenic, Mum had received a brilliant message from a medium called Mark Brandist. The final thing Mark had told her was that Nigel would be all right until he was 30 years old, and then things would change. Prophetic words indeed!

Steadily, as time passed, I came to realise that it wasn't really about me and how *I* felt, but about my brother and how *he* felt. I suppose that, for him, everything had become too much and he just couldn't face life any more. I know that Nigel had great faith and belief in the spirit world – he had been involved within the Spiritualist movement for many years – and he trusted his faith. It's as simple as that.

Waiting for a message

On the Sunday after Nigel's death, I was booked to take my first service at Mexborough Spiritualist church near Doncaster. Everything went well, but I felt as if my heart had been torn out, and I only just managed to get through the work without bursting into tears. Looking back now, I find it slightly uncanny that my first service during that traumatic time was taken in the very same church where Paul had taken his first service as a medium – especially as I was about to enter a very new stage in my life and my mediumship.

I often ask Nigel to come and help me with my work – especially if it is a particularly large demonstration in a theatre. Anyone who has seen me work live will know that I often mention Nigel whilst I am working, more often than not when I am delivering a message from someone who has taken their own life, as this is when I feel his presence most strongly around me.

After he passed I went through a period of wondering how I could possibly go out to Spiritualist churches and give messages from the spirit world to other people when I felt so terribly sad. I was in great need of a message myself. It took a great deal of courage to overcome this particular barrier.

I did honour my bookings, but I didn't really have much heart in my work. I was still hoping for some further contact from Nigel, and I desperately wanted a substantial message for my mum as well. She had taken Nigel's death really badly, and couldn't accept that she had done everything she could for him, and in no way had she let him down. So we took to visiting churches in our spare time, joining the congregations, hoping and praying that one day another medium would be able to relay the message we were so desperate to hear.

No turning back

Quite by chance, we heard that Paul Norton was doing a special service at Lincoln Spiritualist church in July, and decided to go along.

Five of us crammed ourselves into Mum's car. Mum, Brian (Mum's husband), my daughter Gemma, Linda Tideswell (my sister Lisa's mother-in-law) and me. As always, Mum was running late, and we knew we were taking a huge chance; Paul was extremely popular so there might not be any seats left.

We got there just in the nick of time, and managed to sneak into the packed church just as the service was about to start. There were only a few seats left – two right at the back of the church, and three behind a pillar. Mum and Brian went to the back of the church, and Linda, Gemma and I squeezed in behind a pillar. We couldn't see very much.

Paul's first message was excellent, but I cannot remember it for the life of me, probably because what followed was what we had been praying for – a message from Nigel.

Paul started pacing up and down, and stated that he needed to find someone in the congregation who could understand a connection with the surname of Foster. He continued, 'I've got a young man here who is making me aware that he jumped in front of a train.'

At this point, my mum was on the edge of her seat as I looked across, and nodded at her to put her hand up.

'Who's Foster?' he asked.

'Dr Foster was my son's GP,' Mum replied.

'Well, your son says he liked him a lot,' said Paul, 'and there were other doctors he was in contact with as well.'

Mum was nodding away to confirm what he said, but was overcome with emotion, so couldn't really answer.

'You were upset because you weren't able to see him in his coffin.' Mum burst into tears: what Paul had said was quite correct.

'Your son is talking about music, Lisa, and singing,' Paul continued.

'Yes, Lisa is my daughter, and Nigel used to play for her when she sang in pubs,' Mum replied.

'He's talking about trains. I know he was killed by one – but he's talking about a gentleman in the spirit world who also has a connection with trains,' Paul said.

'Yes,' Mum replied, 'My dad used to work on the railways.'

'Well, your son is with his grandad,' said Paul.

Then: 'Who's Charlie?' he asked.

'His other grandad,' Mum replied.

'Well, Charlie is there as well,' said Paul. 'He's OK. You've got to stop worrying about him. He knows about your tears, and the tablets you're taking. You've got to calm down, love – he's all right.'

Paul paced up and down a bit and looked over to where I was sitting. 'Are you connected to this lady?' he asked.

'Yes,' I replied, puzzled.

'Well, for some reason, he wants to thank you for the night he died – somehow you must have helped him.' I nodded in agreement, but was too overcome to answer properly.

'He says you mustn't give up – there's something you must do, something you can't really get out of, but you've been thinking of giving it all up. Well, you mustn't.'

Paul ended the message there, but we had certainly got what we came for. I looked over to Mum: she was crying, but she was happy – she had heard from Nigel. As I looked at her, I realised this was what mediumship was all about – relieving the pain, taking away the heartache, giving bereaved people the will to go on.

That night at Lincoln, Paul went on to give about three other messages, all well received, and he left the platform to a standing ovation. I had to admit we had just witnessed the work of a very fine medium and I thought how much I would love to be able to work to his standard.

I knew, from that moment onwards, that I wouldn't give up because I had a job to do, and I couldn't let down the spirit people, Nigel, or all the people out there who needed me. It was only about a week after this that I returned to Worksop

Spiritualist church. The year was up, and the spirit world had not given up on me. They had kept their side of the bargain, as I had mine. There was no turning back now.

Not taking no for an answer

Life gradually got back to some kind of normality, and one night in August 2001 I decided to go along to Mum's church on the spur of the moment. When I arrived, Mum was standing excitedly at the door.

'Paul Norton is here,' she said.

'Where?' I asked.

'Outside, look, in the black car,' she replied.

I looked over to where she was pointing. Sure enough, there he was, sitting in his car, having a cigarette. When he had finished, he came in and sat down at the back of the church. His friend Daz was with him.

Eventually I plucked up enough courage to walk over to him and blurt out, 'Hi, we saw you at Lincoln – you were brilliant.'

We immediately fell into conversation, and I was amazed at how easy Paul was to talk to. He offered to pass my number on to some of the churches he visited, and I offered to do the same for him, so we exchanged telephone numbers.

A couple of days later, I came home from a shopping trip to find a message on my answering machine. It was from Paul, asking me to give him a call. I did, and again we had a lengthy chat about our work as mediums amongst other things. After that, Paul rang me often. He knew about my inner struggle to regain my confidence in my abilities after Nigel had died, and gave me lots of positive encouragement.

Shortly afterwards, Paul asked if I would be interested in working with him in some public demonstrations. But I was appalled – I could think of a million reasons why working with Paul wouldn't ever be possible, so I turned him down. What he didn't realise at the time was that not only was I struggling with my emotions, but I still lacked confidence. I also had to think about my children and I knew that my husband wouldn't support me if I chose to work with Paul. Our marriage was close to collapse by this point and we were only staying together because neither of us had the strength to call it a day. I knew deep down that deciding to work with Paul would have far-reaching consequences, so I stood firm. It was a definite 'no'.

However, when Paul sets his mind on something he doesn't take no for an answer. We had many heated discussions over the next couple of months and he couldn't seem to understand why I was so reluctant to work with him. His own faith in the spirit world was so great that he believed any problems could easily be overcome.

Another message from Nigel

One night, Paul and I were discussing this issue on the phone yet again. We were going round and round in circles, not really getting anywhere, when suddenly Paul told me that Nigel was with him. At that time Paul lived 21 miles away from me in Doncaster. It was about 10 p.m. and I was a little shocked at what he had just said. I waited anxiously to see what would happen next.

Paul then told me, 'He's showing me a mobile phone in a red case, and he's telling me that he used it before he died.

He's saying that only one trainer was recovered after he was hit, and this was given back to your mum with his watch, which was smashed.'

Everything Paul was saying was correct, and I urged him to continue.

'He's giving me the date of 24th to 25th of May.'

The 24th was the anniversary of Nigel's death and the 25th was his birthday. Then Paul said: 'Also, 2nd of June – someone's birthday was spoilt because of his death.'

My birthday is the 2nd of June.

'He's also talking about a birthday in January.'

This was my mum's birthday.

'And a birthday in September,' (my sister's), 'and a birthday in November,' (my brother's).

'Who's Tony?' Paul asked.

My dad, I responded, feeling very excited. Because this information was all so pertinent, it could only be Nigel who was giving it.

'He's telling me about his computer and his keyboard being kept in a box in an upstairs room. There's CDs, hundreds and hundreds of CDs. Some of them are what Nigel wrote and recorded himself – demos and stuff.' I wasn't sure about this and said I would have to check. 'He's talking about a birthday – there were birthday presents left unopened. One of them is a tankard.' Again, I said I would have to check this out.

Paul went on to mention the name of Carol (one of Nigel's former girlfriends) and Darren (her little boy). He wanted to send love to his mum and to thank her for the funeral, as she had played rock music at it instead of church music and Nigel thought this was funny. He then went on to describe the place where his death had happened, mentioning a bridge over a road, an embankment and a heavy goods train, coal, etc. All this was completely accurate. Nigel threw himself in front of a heavy goods train just past a bridge, near an embankment.

Then Paul became slightly confused – 'I think he's talking about somewhere called Eagle,' he said. I confirmed that Nigel's address had been Eagle Place. Paul went on to describe Nigel's flat in such perfect detail that I couldn't believe what I was hearing. Throughout the message, little bits of Nigel's humour kept popping up, and I was left in no doubt that it was him coming through.

All in all, this communication lasted about two hours. Bearing in mind that this was done on the telephone, over a distance of 20 miles, it was an extraordinary demonstration of Paul's ability as a medium.

Afterwards, I had the best night's sleep I had had in ages. When I woke the next morning, my mind was clearer and I felt as if a huge weight had been lifted from my shoulders. This message helped in more ways than one. After weeks of denial, I decided that I really wanted to team up with Paul and work alongside him. I rang him to let him know.

In his typical manner, Paul said he had been waiting for my call – and urged that we get down to business straightaway.

I now know that Nigel provided the turning point in my life, which led to me finally becoming Tracy Hall – *the medium*.

Nigel brought me back to Spiritualism by encouraging me to join his healing circle. He introduced me to his friend Chris, who helped me to receive bookings and establish myself in the churches. Most importantly of all, Nigel finally, after all the years of near misses, brought me into contact with Paul.

CHAPTER 14
Paul: With a little help from God...

A week or so after the *Kilroy* programme had been screened I received yet another phone call from Barbara Kelly. Radio 4 were planning a programme called *Ad-Lib*, hosted by Robbie Robertson. The producers had seen me on *Kilroy* and were impressed with what I'd said. They asked Laurie O'Leary to put a group of mediums together to discuss mediumship, and said that they definitely wanted me on the programme.

I arrived at Broadcasting House, London, one cold January morning. Waiting in the foyer was medium Glyn Edwards, and the renowned Gordon Higginson (who was at that time President of the Spiritualists' National Union). Doris Collins was also there. I said hello to them all, shook their hands and nervously went to take a seat. A short time later, Laurie O'Leary came in, accompanied by Danish medium Marion Dampier-Jeans.

We were then taken over to a studio in another building, where we were introduced to Robert (Robbie) Robinson, who used to host a television show called *Ask the Family.* I remembered watching it when I was younger.

Robbie explained that he wanted us all to discuss

mediumship, and he would occasionally ask questions. It all seemed pretty clear and I felt comfortable and relaxed.

Robbie started by asking where the spirit world was and how it worked. Gordon Higginson explained the various states of consciousness, and Doris added that she wasn't exactly sure how it worked for her, but she was aware that it worked very well indeed. When Robbie suggested that maybe some of the messages were a little trivial, I interrupted and explained that the spirit people were not necessarily going to talk about major events just because they had passed over to the other side, unless, of course, they were the type of people who had always been interested in such affairs. Because they retained the same personality when they joined the spirit world, they were more likely to talk about ordinary day-to-day situations that some people might find mundane.

To illustrate what I had said, Doris told Robbie a story about a sitting she'd given to an American lady, emphasising that what appeared to be a mundane message to other people turned out to be quite remarkable for the lady concerned, as it had apparently transformed her whole life.

Robbie was still quite inquisitive about it all and asked whether or not we felt we should deliver predictions. Marion Dampier-Jeans said that this should not be done in a Spiritualist church but sometimes it was acceptable in private sittings, where there could be a need. Gordon Higginson added that this was called psychism and not mediumship.

Gordon then spoke a little bit about physical mediumship, where spirit people could manifest themselves quite visibly to those present and their voices could be audible to everyone.

Robbie seemed a little taken aback by this but accepted Gordon's explanation.

The interview went on for well over an hour and we'd all thoroughly enjoyed discussing our various experiences and giving our opinions. Laurie had arranged the group so that there was a mixture of young and not-so-young mediums, and this worked well, giving people the opportunity to hear both traditional and newer points of view.

When the programme was broadcast on Radio 4, it was obvious that they'd edited it quite a bit. Nevertheless, it all sounded very good. Of course, by this time, I was getting quite used to speaking on television and radio, and I felt I had come across quite confidently.

In at the deep end

I was extremely pleased when, a short time later I was invited by Gordon Higginson to take part in the week-long advanced mediumship course at Stansted Hall, also known as The Arthur Findlay college.

The building had been left to the Spiritualists' Union by Arthur Findlay, who wanted it to be used for spiritual advancement. Regular courses for developing mediums and healers are held there, and Gordon was Principal of the college.

This was a really positive period in my work as a medium. In the weeks that followed I eagerly looked forward to my visit to Stansted Hall, where I hoped to learn more and become a better medium, under Gordon's watchful eye.

When I arrived at the college, I was impressed with the scenery and the beautiful old building, where I would be staying for the next week. I made my way to the main entrance and there, sitting on one of the benches, was a rather sad-looking lady.

'Hello,' I said, smiling.

I assumed she was one of the lecturers but I couldn't help feeling that she seemed a little upset, so I sent a thought out to the spirit world for her to receive the help she needed.

As I entered the building, I saw Glyn Edwards in the foyer. He came rushing over to shake my hand and took hold of one of my bags and directed me to my room. After dinner, we all met in the library. There, Glyn introduced us all to each other and explained that Gordon would be arriving late on Sunday evening. He went on to discuss the week's events, after which most of the students made their way to the bar.

We then had to go upstairs to the mediums' lounge to divide the students into groups. Gordon had left instructions that I was to shadow Glyn so that he could show me how the lecturers worked. I had thought I was going along to Stansted to participate in the course as a student. As it turned out, Gordon wanted me to spend the week teaching others and lecturing (provided I was at the required standard, that is). When I found this out, I was very nervous indeed, especially when Gordon arrived on Sunday evening.

He was a man who, as I found out later, had a habit of dropping things on you at the last minute. He told me that I would be required to do some 'test sittings' to make sure that my mediumship was of a good standard.

As it turned out, I had five sittings to undertake. The first lady was from Switzerland, and her father communicated a very nice message to her. The second sitting I did was for a

Swedish lady called Annika Langlet. She didn't say very much at all and her face seemed expressionless. At the end of the sitting I just smiled and asked, 'I hope it's been all right for you?'

'Yes, it was very good indeed,' came her reply. I was relieved – she seemed very impressed.

After that, I saw a couple of English people. In fact, they had both come from Yorkshire, so we had much in common and were able to have a chat about the area afterwards.

Strangely enough, the last appointment I had was with the lady I'd said hello to on my way into the college on my first day there. As she entered the room, she still looked quite sad. I started the sitting and immediately sensed a young man of about 18 years old, who wished to communicate. As it turned out, this was the lady's son, who told me he had been killed in a car crash in Bombay, India. As I told her all the information I could about his death, she started to cry.

It was a particularly remarkable sitting because I couldn't speak a word of his language, and so, now and again, when I couldn't get my tongue around the words, I would ask him to spell them. He managed to tell me his name and nickname, and other personal details about himself and other family members. Afterwards I felt the need to give the lady a big hug. As I did so, she was able to stop crying for a few moments.

She then told me that she felt, for those few seconds when I hugged her, that it was her son who had held her, and this is what had stopped her from crying. She went on to say that other mediums had given her a message from him, but that no one had been able to give his name or nickname. She was so overwhelmed with the comfort she had derived from the sitting that it was quite a humbling experience for me to be with her.

I couldn't thank the spirit world enough for helping me to get through the sittings. Gordon had heard about some of the messages, and he was pleased to hear that I had done a good job.

'I knew you would do well, Paul,' he said, quite knowingly.

On television again

That same week the BBC were filming an *Open Space* programme about the college and Spiritualism. Gordon was to be filmed demonstrating his work in the main hall used for demonstrations at Stansted, known as the sanctuary. This is a beautiful space, which can comfortably seat around 200 people. At one end of the room there are magnificent stained-glass windows which enable the light to stream through, creating an almost ethereal atmosphere. Right at the last minute, he decided that Glyn, myself and another medium would join him on the platform.

My nerves went into overdrive at the prospect of doing a televised demonstration! I wasn't sure which was the most nerve-racking – being filmed by the TV crew or demonstrating in front of Gordon. Everyone knew he was a brilliant medium – so much so that within Spiritualist circles his nickname was 'God'.

To make matters worse, the sanctuary was packed full, and I had to sit right next to Gordon on the platform. I didn't think I was going to be able to manage a single word, let alone a full-blown message from the spirit world!

I was chosen to go first, and fortunately the message I was able to give was quite good. In fact, once I had overcome my terrible nerves, I was sure I could have carried on if they'd allowed me to. Unfortunately there wasn't enough time.

The Spiritualists' National Union had editorial control over the filming so I knew that the finished product was likely to give a reasonably positive impression of the work of mediums, and of Spiritualism in general.

The rest of the week flew by, and on the last day Gordon came to see me.

'Now Paul, you'll be all right for Mediumship 2000 Week, won't you?'

I was shocked by what he'd said, and also slightly confused.

'Pardon?' I replied.

'You *are* going to come along?' He wasn't so much asking me as telling me I was going to be there.

'Well, er...' I stammered, 'I'll need to make arrangements for Daz.'

'Good,' he said. 'That's settled then.'

An exciting invitation

When I returned to the college for three days during Mediumship 2000 week, Gordon had given me a very big build-up. He'd mentioned how I had appeared on the television and radio, about the article that had been in the *Sunday Mirror* magazine, and also said that he personally thought that I was a very good medium. This all meant that, when I arrived, there was a bit of a buzz, and quite a few people wanted to know more about me.

There were more tutors available to work that week, so I spent my time moving from class to class. On my last evening, Gordon had arranged for me to give a demonstration in the library with two other mediums. Once again, he gave me a marvellous build-up at the start of the evening.

'Paul is a very good medium,' he said, adding humorously, 'but not as good as some of us.' The audience found this highly amusing.

Before I left the college that evening, Gordon collared me in the foyer. 'I want you to come to the Physical Mediumship Week in Stansted,' he said.

'Really?' I asked.

'Yes, of course,' he replied. 'Now do you think you can make it for the whole week?'

'I'll certainly do my best,' I said, eagerly.

'Well, I'll give you a call in a few days to arrange everything,' he replied.

Physical Phenomena Week, as it was officially called, was very popular and always fully booked because Gordon would often give a demonstration of physical mediumship. This meant that he would go into a trance-like state, and then, if the conditions were correct, the spirit people would materialise themselves for everyone to see. The materialised spirit form would then be able to move about and speak to the audience. I'd only ever read about such phenomena and, although I found the idea of it quite amazing, I wasn't certain that I believed it was possible.

The invitation to attend the week was a very exciting opportunity for me to witness some of the most remarkable mediumship ever demonstrated, and I will be eternally grateful to

Gordon for thinking of me, and for allowing me to be present for such a prestigious event.

Eventually the date came around. When I arrived at the college I was greeted by Muriel Tennant and Eileen Mitchumson, two of the other mediums.

On the Sunday evening, Gordon approached me in the dining room. 'You'll be doing the service tonight,' he said, giving me only an hour's notice before it was due to begin.

I didn't have time to think, let alone panic, and in next to no time, I found myself standing on the platform in front of a sea of faces. The sanctuary was packed full.

When it came to the last message, the communication seemed to start off very well and then it slowly began to fade. To fill in a little, I glanced at Gordon, and then, turning back to the audience, asked, 'Do you ever get the feeling that you are being watched by God?' Everyone found this very amusing, including Gordon himself.

My little joke lifted the atmosphere and I was soon able to finish off the message.

After the service that night, one gentleman, Mike Scott, came up and said that he thought my work was very good indeed. As Gordon told me later, he very much respected Mike for his honesty and knowledge, and if Mike had complimented me then my work must have been very good.

A very memorable demonstration

The highlight of the week was Thursday evening, when Gordon had agreed to give a demonstration of physical mediumship.

Before he started, he was thoroughly searched by a couple of students chosen at random. He did this as a matter of course in order to dispel any suggestion of underhand practices. He wore a loose-fitting shirt, a pair of trousers and some slippers. Everyone attending the meeting had been asked to remove items of a metallic nature and they were checked for tape recorders and cameras. This was to ensure there would be no sudden noises, which might be harmful to Gordon when he was in a trance state.

I had been chosen to sit on the platform next to Eileen Mitchumson, alongside the cabinet that Gordon was sitting in. We were not more than twelve inches away from it. Apparently, a small space such as a cabinet is ideal for this type of mediumship, as it enables the power to build up more easily. All the lights were turned out whilst Gordon went into a trance state. After about seven minutes his guide, Choo Chow, came through very strongly indeed. Suddenly there was the sound of clear voices talking simultaneously, then the voice of Cuckoo, another of Gordon's helpers, stood out above all others.

'Paul,' she said quite clearly. 'You'd better come and get this.'

I looked at Eileen; she nodded. Shaking a little, I stood up, turned towards the cabinet and leaned forwards. I could clearly see Gordon in a deep state of trance with his hands clasped together, resting on his stomach. There was no movement from him at all. I heard a rustle and then the clinking of metal. Right before my eyes, I could see Gordon's belt coming off his trousers, with the buckle end (which was quite large) going through each eye last.

There was no doubt that the spirits were taking his belt off! As it came out towards me, I held my hands closer. It was like a steel rule, a solid form, and as I reached out, the belt coiled up into my hands. I shuddered in amazement. Later, I remembered that physical mediums are not supposed to wear any form of metal whilst demonstrating. This is because the power that is generated is so intense that it can cause injury to them.

As I returned to my seat, there were muffled voices, which soon started to get clearer. They seemed to echo in the whole room and were not coming from any particular direction. As they got louder, a faint glow began to appear near Gordon's neck, and grew larger and larger, flowing to the floor like some kind of smoke or fog. This substance is known as ectoplasm. Slowly the mist continued to flow, eventually building up into the distinct form of a spirit person.

It turned out to be a man. He started to talk in his own dialect to his wife, who was seated in the audience, giving absolutely marvellous and detailed information to her about their life together. I was deeply moved by the whole experience. Whilst at first I couldn't believe my eyes, I was dumbfounded by the importance of what I was privileged to be witnessing. The spirit person's voice echoed throughout the library.

As the séance continued, other spirit people materialised. Some were clearer than others. An American lady received a message from her brother who had passed over. He gave full names and addresses from the past. His American accent was exceptionally clear and precise. He spoke of their mother's illness, giving the exact location and name of the hospital she was in, in New York. He then broke the news to his sister that their mother would be joining him the following March.

From start to finish, the whole séance was truly remarkable. Afterwards poor Gordon was so exhausted that he had to go straight to bed.

A few weeks later, just after Christmas, I spoke to Gordon. He told me he'd been unwell over the holiday and he was due to work in Blackpool over the weekend but didn't feel up to going.

'I shall have to go, though,' he said. 'I can't let them down.' We ended the conversation by saying that we would see each other in early February for the first weekend course of the year.

Sadly, Gordon passed over to the spirit world a few days later. He'd returned from Blackpool and, at around lunchtime, had a heart attack and passed away. His physical presence is still missed by many. Gordon worked tirelessly for the spirit world, travelling in this country and abroad. He will always be remembered for his tremendous efforts on behalf of Spiritualism, along with many other pioneers who have gone before him.

That last week at Stansted, working alongside Gordon and witnessing the materialisation, meant a great deal to me. I believe this episode in my life was yet another one that was engineered by fate. Often I feel that I was guided to that séance; after all, if I hadn't met Gordon at the radio station,

I might never have been invited to go to Stansted. Gordon Higginson was one of the best Spiritualist mediums who ever lived and the fact that he was willing to assist me to develop my own gifts proved to me that I really was destined to do this work.

Catching up on other aspects of life

There were times during these early years when I questioned where it was all leading, but something always seemed to turn up to point me in the right direction, and my mediumship progressed at a steady pace. In fact, I had achieved an awful lot in a very short time, and there was a point in the mid-1990s when I wondered if I had done too much too soon, and I began to wonder what the future held.

I had put so much into my mediumship, helping other people and looking after Daz, that I began to feel slightly resentful. I felt I had given up the best years of my life (my late teens and early twenties) to a tiring and often emotionally draining job. Yes, I had travelled and come into contact with some fantastic people, yet still I felt alone. I felt that many of the friendships I had embarked upon were based solely on the fact that people wanted to be around me because of my status as a medium, and the messages they might receive. I personally felt that none of my friends knew me, Paul Norton, the person who loves the countryside, likes nothing more than to have a good laugh, and who is thirsty for new skills and information.

It seemed that everyone I had loved who had helped me with my mediumship had left my life – Gordon Higginson,

Doris Collins, Janet Vaughan, Sam and others too numerous to mention. So, badly in need of a rest, I decided to do less mediumship and concentrate on my own life for a while.

I enrolled at university, and spent the next two years studying for a Certificate of Higher Education in Sheffield. I did some voluntary work, and for once in my life had a social life outside Spiritualism. I managed to find reliable carers who were willing to help look after Daz, and I even embarked upon a couple of relationships which were fun while they lasted, but I knew, deep down, that these were not people I could settle down and spend the rest of my life with.

I still did a few church services, as I found I could not let go of Spiritualism altogether. After all, it was such a big part of my life. But I wasn't travelling as much as I had done; I just wanted to live a normal life for a while.

Looking for a partner in mediumship

After university I moved from job to job. However, it was difficult to find something that fitted in with caring for Daz. The carers I hired often used to let me down, which made working for an employer difficult. I soon came to realise that working as a medium had given me a great deal of freedom and autonomy over the years. If people hadn't been available to care for Daz whilst I was a full-time medium, I had just taken him along with me, and so it had all worked perfectly. Eventually, it seemed that returning to mediumship full time was probably my only option.

So, in 1999, I started to accept bookings for charity events again, and began touring on a regular basis. I still felt lonely and yearned for someone new and interesting to talk to. I had met other mediums and tried to form working partnerships with some of them. However, none of those partnerships lasted very long, and often they were more problematic than I had anticipated. I still wanted to work with someone else but I had more or less given up hoping to meet someone who was on the same wavelength as me.

From time to time, I heard about new mediums that were doing well and I would take an interest in them. In the year 2000, one name kept coming up over and over again. That name was Tracy Hall.

Do you believe in fate? If anyone had asked me this question 20 years ago I would have said no. However, now I'm not so sure. When I met Tracy on 17 August 2001 it was at a time in my life when I really needed a friend.

A few weeks earlier, on a glorious Sunday afternoon at the end of July, my good friends of 13 years, Gail and Paul Buckley, invited Daz and I to visit Harrogate Spiritualist church. When we set off we didn't know who the medium would be, but it turned out to be a really nice lady from Bradford. We joined the congregation, and after the customary hymns, prayer and philosophy, the medium started her demonstration.

She began by describing a gentleman in the spirit world who had passed away, following a heart attack, whose name was Gordon. No one responded. She then pointed directly at me.

'This gentleman,' she continued, 'tells me that he suffered from leg ulcers and also diabetes, and that you knew him quite well.'

Suddenly, it all clicked into place. Gordon Higginson had

passed away with a heart attack, very suddenly. He had also suffered from terrible leg ulcers and diabetes during his life. I was very taken aback, and felt slightly honoured that I was about to receive a message from my dear friend and teacher Gordon.

'He tells me that he helped you once before and that he'll do the same again, only this time from the other side.'

I wasn't really sure what she meant.

'He's concerned that you are far too trusting of people and he says that you must be careful for you are shortly to be betrayed.' She paused to think for a moment before continuing. 'You will be let down by someone very close indeed. This gentleman says you are not to worry – he will give you the strength and courage to go forward and overcome these obstacles.'

I looked first at Daz, and then at Paul and Gail.

'You are about to enter a new phase in your life, and you will shortly meet someone who will hold your hand every step of the way.'

Then the medium moved on to the next person.

During the message, I noticed that the medium had even displayed some of Gordon's mannerisms and traits, so I knew her message was likely to be quite correct. I don't like to dwell on negatives, but I admit that all through the rest of the service I could not get those thoughts out of my head. On the way home very little was said about what had happened.

However, a few days later, I had a massive argument with Paul and obviously Gail was drawn in as well. The argument was over something quite trivial, but things were said which caused irreparable damage to our friendship. I was now lonelier than ever.

A new life begins

Only a few weeks later, I once again made a last-minute decision to travel out to a Spiritualist church. This time I decided to visit Retford, where an old acquaintance Janice Jackson, who I had known for years, was president. This was where destiny finally intervened. In all the years I had known Janice, I hadn't realised she had a daughter. That night, I met a new friend – Tracy Hall.

I had never met anyone quite like Tracy before and was intrigued by her vibrant personality and enthusiasm for life. Over the coming weeks and months I discovered that she was one of the kindest and most caring people I had ever met. Nothing was ever too much trouble for her, and she had a brilliant rapport with Daz, so we immediately became the best of friends. Her knowledge of mediumship impressed me, but I soon came to realise that she suffered from a deep lack of confidence. She confided that this was because she had suffered a nervous breakdown, and still had trouble with her self-esteem. For some reason, which I could never understand, she had real issues about her appearance and hated meeting new people. The thought of standing up in front of an audience terrified her.

Nevertheless, she faced her demons head on, and was working really hard in the Spiritualist churches and at charity events when I first met her. She was also extremely intelligent; in fact she could be described as intellectual. This aspect of her personality fascinated me – here was someone who not only shared my interest in mediumship, but who could hold her own in a challenging debate about many different subjects. In the past I had found that some of my friends' interests and hobbies were not exactly my cup of tea, and the only thing we had in common was that they would often want messages and I could give them. To meet someone like Tracy who was around my own age, with a similar background and an enquiring mind, just seemed too good to be true! She never sought messages or asked for anything other than companionship.

We became inseparable, our friendship grew, and although I didn't realise it at the time, I was falling for her in a big way.

Little did I realise that the message I had received at Harrogate from Gordon would actually affect Tracy as well – that she was the one who would hold my hand and lead me to a very different life. In fact my life was to become quite the opposite of the one I had lived for the past 16 years.

CHAPTER 15
Tracy: The hand of destiny

When Paul and I first met and started to get to know one another, we realised that we had too many similarities in our lives for them to have occurred just by chance. It seemed as though we had always been destined to meet, but the timing had never been right.

At that time Paul and Daz were in the process of moving to a flat in Doncaster – number 11 Auckland Road. I lived at 11 Auckland Road, Retford. Paul had previously lived in a three storey-house in Doncaster; I had owned a three-storey-house in Retford. Paul's father took his own life; my brother also took his own life. Paul has a brother called Tony; my dad was called Tony. Paul's grandparents lived at Lidget Lane near Barnsley; my mum lived on a street just off Lidget Lane in Retford. I worked in a Jobcentre for 13 years; Paul also worked in a Jobcentre for a while. Paul worked at a night-club called 'Seventh Heaven' in Doncaster, and while he was working there, I used to go to the club every week with my friends from work. Paul's birthday is 6 November; this was my Grandad Jackson's birthday. Paul had been acquainted with my mum for many years and he'd telephoned her on the day my Grandad Carter died. He was one of four children, and so

239

was I. Paul's nickname for his dog Gyp was 'Pippin'; my dog was called 'Pippin', which we shortened to Pip.

There are other coincidences too numerous to mention, all of which led us to believe that we were brought together for a reason. That reason was to team up together and unite with the spirit world, to share our experiences with other people and to help them through their own pain.

Breaking up

When I first started working with Paul in 2000, I was still married to my first husband. However, we had grown apart over a number of years, and there were terrible rifts in our marriage. At the beginning of 2002, my husband had been offered a new job, which would have meant moving to Nottingham. At this point, I had just started to establish myself as a professional medium, so I said no. I had been working with Paul for about three months, and didn't want to give up a wonderful opportunity to make something of my life. My husband didn't like my association with Paul and was very unsupportive of my work. He wanted me to give it all up and go back to being a 'normal' housewife and mother.

We were unable to resolve our differences and eventually agreed to divorce. In all honesty, the 16 years we had been married were unhappy ones for me. I felt that my husband didn't care for me as I would have liked him to. He seemed far more interested in football and computers than he did in building bridges in our relationship. Our marriage had been a volatile one right from the beginning. The truth of the matter was that we married too young, and we had grown up and grown apart during the years we had been together. I had known deep within me for many years that I was unhappy in this relationship.

When I left my first husband in June 2002, Paul kindly helped me to find a part-time job in an estate agency so that I would be able to support myself and my two children; he also helped me to find somewhere to live. When I discovered that Dad had cancer, he was the one who offered to look after the kids for me whilst I rushed backwards and forwards to the hospice and nursing home, and tried to juggle my dad's care with part-time work, demonstrations of mediumship and motherhood.

In December 2002, just after my dad had died, my ex-husband decided he wanted our children to go back to Retford to live with him. I was very reluctant to let them go, but knew my husband was determined to have them back, so I asked Gemma and Luke what they wanted to do. They had been staying regularly with their Dad and his new girlfriend, who also had two children of similar ages to them. I knew they enjoyed the feeling of being part of a family again, and that they preferred the more affluent lifestyle their father was able to provide, so I wasn't shocked when they told me they wanted to return to Retford. I was so tired and exhausted – I had just ended my marriage, moved home and lost my dad – too much had happened in too short a space of time. I didn't have the energy to oppose these plans, so Gemma and Luke stayed with their dad for three and a half years, but they now live with me full-time. I kept in constant touch with them whilst they were living with their father, and saw them regularly, but grieved for them every minute of every day that they were not with me, and found the strain of not having them unbearable.

I felt guilty about wanting to end my marriage, but I have always wanted the best not just for me, but for my ex-husband and my children. He took the divorce very badly, and unfortunately he still bears a grudge towards me for wanting a better and more fulfilling life for myself. Sadly, we are no longer on speaking terms.

Changing feelings

The one person who helped me to cope with everything was Paul. It was whilst my dad was ill in 2002 that I realised I was growing to care for him in a way which was more than just friendship, but I kept my feelings to myself.

That is – until my dad died. When I returned home from clearing out Dad's flat, Paul immediately telephoned me, asking me to commit to plans to do more work together. I was still grieving, and was in all honesty trying not to become too involved with him so that I could keep my feelings for him hidden and under control. Eventually we ended up having an awful row about it all.

I don't know why I did it, but immediately after putting the phone down, I sent him an email explaining that my feelings for him were growing into more than just friendship, but I knew he didn't think of me in that way, and in any case I wasn't good enough for him. I told him I felt the only option for me was to give up the mediumship and return to Retford.

Shortly after opening my email, Paul telephoned me. He said everything I expected him to – that he didn't think it was a good idea, that he valued my friendship too much, and that there was work to think about. Basically, he was giving me the brush-off.

'It's not that I don't find you attractive, because I do – I think you're lovely,' he told me, before we ended the conversation.

Of course I was upset, but I accepted his decision, and started to make plans to move back home to Retford.

The next few days were difficult. We had joint work commitments, and so we naturally had to spend time together. I was determined to keep our meetings more businesslike, and was careful not to be over-familiar with Paul. On the Thursday after my dad died, I was round at Paul's house helping to design a new poster, and he was trying to entice me to come over to lunch at his house on Sunday.

Since I had lived in Doncaster we had taken it in turns to have lunch at each other's houses every weekend. One week I would cook, the next Paul. After what had happened, I no longer felt this was appropriate, and so I flatly refused his invitation. He was quite shocked that I was so determined and questioned me about what I would do instead. I said I had made plans to go Christmas shopping, and that I would just grab a sandwich or something for lunch. He tried to persuade me to call in and see him, but I became upset and told him he was being unfair under the circumstances, and that he would have to get used to spending less time with me.

He went quiet for a while, and then stood up and lit a cigarette.

'Well,' he said, 'I suppose we could give it a try.'

My mouth went dry, and my heart was pounding as I looked over at him. I didn't dare to hope that Paul was suggesting we try a relationship, so I didn't speak, just waited for him to continue.

'Look, Tracy,' he said, 'the thought of not having you around really scares me.' He took my hand. 'I've loved having you as a friend this past year, and my feelings for you have also grown, but I suppose I was so keen to succeed with our work that I pushed my feelings aside.'

I tried to pull my hand away.

'No, don't,' he said, 'Please listen. If we have a relationship, and it doesn't work, we risk losing everything, but I'm prepared to take that risk if you are.'

I was tearful as I agreed with him to give it a try and see how things went. Later I discovered that Paul had been trying to invite me to lunch on Sunday so he could prepare a lovely romantic meal and ask me out properly. Trust me to mess things up again!

Becoming a couple

Making the transition from being 'just friends' to becoming a couple was easy as we had spent so much time together during the past year that in many ways we were already like an old married couple.

In January 2003, Paul persuaded me to give up the lease on my rented house, and I moved in with him and Daz. We soon settled into each other's company. Paul and I cared for Daz together, and I kept in constant touch with Gemma and Luke, spending time with them whenever I could. I spoilt Daz rotten, probably mothering him because I didn't have my children, and, after the last couple of difficult years, I started to feel settled again. Our work was going from strength to strength, and we were now working in theatres rather than community centres. Everywhere we went, our work was very well received. It seemed as though we could start looking towards the future.

In March 2003, we travelled to Sheffield to watch a special demonstration of mediumship with Gerard Smith at Clarkson Street Spiritualist church. He pointed directly at me, stating that he had a gentleman with him who had hanged himself. I nervously told him that the contact might be for Paul, who was sitting next to me. Gerard continued to speak to both of us together. Daz was also there that night, sitting to the left of Paul.

'This gentleman tells me that he never actually met you when he was alive – but somehow you have introduced yourself to him since.'

I couldn't quite believe the accuracy of this, because, only a few days before, Paul had taken me to Rosehill Cemetery in Doncaster, where his dad's memorial stone was. In my mind I had sent a thought out to Paul's dad and asked him for his blessing on our relationship.

Gerard then pointed to Paul.

'He is giving you a shield for protection,' he said. 'He tells me that you will need this shield over the coming months, and that you are to think of him when things become really difficult, and he will be there.'

After he had made this statement, he looked directly at Daz, and then back at Paul and me. He ended by saying, 'He gives the two of you his blessing.'

We weren't quite sure what he meant about the shield, but we were soon to find out.

Painful changes

Only two weeks later, at the end of March, Paul and I had gone out to look at a venue and arrange a booking. Whilst we were gone, Daz, supported and encouraged by Paul's friend Maureen, went to the local authority and decided to place himself in care. He has never offered any explanation as to why he did this but we can only assume that he was unhappy about Paul's relationship with me, and the fact that our work together was really taking off. He certainly had no need to feel this way, because Paul and I included him in everything we did, and his actions came as a real shock to us. By August 2003, our lives were almost in tatters.

The fact that Daz no longer wanted Paul to be his carer meant that their house, which they jointly owned, had to be sold. I began to wish I hadn't given up my rented house after all. We were left virtually penniless and on the verge of home-lessness as solicitors and social services stepped in and froze all the joint bank accounts pending their enquiries. Daz had made some awful allegations against us. Even more shock-ingly, all Paul's friends seemed to support him in his actions. Many of them took Daz's side. It took us just over a year to put together all the paperwork required to disprove the claims that had been made. We handed this information over to Daz's solicitor, and eventually he admitted that what he had said had been untrue. We couldn't understand why everyone – especially Daz, seemed to be so against our relationship, and it seemed to be another peculiar coincidence that both of us lost the people we had cared for and looked after during that painful period in our lives. It was almost as if we were having to start again from the beginning, and all our past lives had to be erased in order for us to do so. It was a really strange and difficult experience for us to go through, but at least we had each other.

In her book, *The Power Within*, Doris Collins wrote:

'If you decide to follow the path of service, you may find that the way will be hard and that you will lose many friends in consequence, but so long as your conscience is quite clear, it matters not. If you have a destiny to fulfil, the right people will be drawn to you in a miraculous way, and although you may hesitate at the crossroad, uncertain which direction to take, you will be shown the right path.'

To us, Doris's words provide further confirmation that our meeting cannot be put down to chance. It seems as if we found each other at just the right time – a time when old friendships were coming to an end. Somehow our getting together caused a series of events in both our lives that we wouldn't necessarily have wanted to happen. However, we do have clear consciences. And the very fact that we are now successful at the work we do makes us sure that we have been guided and placed on the right path together.

We continued to do the meetings we had already booked, but it was difficult to do the work when our home life was in such a muddle. In August 2003, just as we were at our lowest, we went to Retford Town Hall. Two hundred tickets had been sold, and we really felt that we couldn't let people down. It was an excellent night, and we gave a message to a lady called Lynn, who had recently lost her father. She later sent us the following email:

Dear Paul and Tracy,

Just a quick note to thank you for the lovely evening last night at Retford.

I was the one whom you kindly answered the question as to whether my Father would have known I missed his passing. Paul … You were Soooooooooo accurate when you explained about me getting stuck in traffic and my sister being with me. I DID lean on his head and whisper in his ear – he DID have brown leathery skin, as Tracy described and loved sitting in his garden. BUT IT WAS THE CHIP SHOP THAT DID IT!

I now feel EXTREMELY relieved to know that he joined me in the car that morning before passing over, and I did feel dizzy and I also felt exactly the same last night.

My sister was with me last night, she had not seen a clairvoyant before and she was fascinated by what you did.

For the first time in a long time I had a good night's sleep. Thank you Paul and Tracy, I really appreciate it. KEEP IT UP!!

Lynn

For better or worse...

In October 2003, we were lucky enough to get a three-bedroomed flat at Bradway in Sheffield, right on the edge of the beautiful Derbyshire countryside. It had previously been owned by a very old lady, and so it needed a great deal of work. We spent every day there stripping wallpaper and painting and decorating. One afternoon, we were collapsed in a heap on the floor, having a well-earned tea break, when Paul became very serious and took my hand.

'Tracy,' he said, 'I'm certain that you're the person I want to spend the rest of my life with, and I'd be so happy if you would do me the honour of becoming my wife.'

It wasn't the most romantic of settings, but Paul's words came from the heart and I immediately said yes. A couple of weeks later, on 6 November, Paul's birthday, we went and bought an engagement ring, and I was happier than I had been in a very long time.

Of course all the upheavals we had encountered did cause a slight setback in our work – but never once affected our love for each other. In fact, if anything, these problems brought us closer together. However, we took the decision to do less mediumship for a while, because it was difficult to be able to help other people when we were feeling so low ourselves. We found part-time jobs to help sort out our financial difficulties. I went to work on a project helping lone parents back to work, whilst Paul got a job working for the Citizens Advice Bureau. We hated our jobs, and spent a lot of time planning when we could go back to working as mediums again.

In January 2005, we agreed to do a telephone sitting for a lady called Josie, who lived in Tasmania, Australia. Sadly, Josie's daughter had died a few months earlier from a brain tumour. We tuned into the energies around us, whilst talking to Josie, who lived thousands of miles away and was waiting anxiously at the end of the telephone for news of her beloved daughter. Once again, the spirit world didn't let us down.

Eleanor – Josie's daughter – came dancing into our vision, and when we relayed this to Josie, she was able to confirm that Eleanor loved dancing. We described the symptoms the little girl had experienced which started her illness, and spoke of the long and arduous journeys to hospital. We talked of the diagnosis and Josie's refusal to accept this, and that she tried hard to get specialist after specialist to look into the case – even writing to consultants in Switzerland and all around Europe. We mentioned the little stripy hat that Eleanor had worn whilst she was undergoing treatment, and the terrible effect the treatment had on her and her family. At the point that I described Eleanor's father carrying her into hospital towards the end of her life because she didn't like to go in a wheelchair, we were all tearful about the evidence that was coming through.

Reaching a wider audience?

This was an amazing experience for us, and one we shall never forget. People like Josie remind us how lucky we are – to be able to reunite those who have been parted, to give them just a few minutes together again to remember each other, and to speak of the wonderful times they have shared. Sometimes these few minutes of communication give a person the strength to go on, and for this gift alone we are truly grateful.

This is why, when we received an invitation to appear on Sky Television, in April 2005, we thought it would give us the opportunity to demonstrate our work to a wider audience and to help a lot of people in the process.

Sadly, that was not the way it turned out.

We were asked to go to Feltham in Middlesex, to appear on a programme that involved members of the general public texting into the studio with requests for psychic or spiritual messages. From 7 p.m. until 2 a.m., we would be giving messages, live on air, to the people who texted in. Initially we received no payment for this work, but towards the end, the TV show agreed to pay our expenses.

When we arrived for our first show, we felt slightly disappointed at the reception we received. We were left waiting in a corridor for around 45 minutes until the company director could speak to us. She then rushed up, and insisted on looking at the outfits we had brought to wear, to see if she thought we would be suitably dressed for the show.

One of the other psychics introduced herself to us, and we were surprised at the advice she offered. 'Don't go into too much detail and keep it vague,' she instructed.

Needless to say, we remained true to ourselves and our work. Luckily, we were very well received, and the studio staff said they had never had so many texts for readings.

The feedback was amazing, and confirmed that everything we had said was correct. Needless to say, the TV people were really impressed and asked us to go back on a regular basis. They even offered us our own weekly spot.

We went along to Middlesex regularly between April and August 2005 to appear on the show. However, as time went on, we both became slightly concerned at the fact that we were encouraged to do short readings for people, rather than go into depth and get things right. We were aware too that many of the TV staff sent in their own texts, and the presenters gave these priority over the paying customers. We didn't feel this was fair, and we also felt that we were being exploited. We had to sit in a tiny studio, answering text after text after text, while the producers of the show kept whispering in the ear of the presenter, telling her to make us hurry up, and keep things moving.

On one occasion, we travelled all the way to Feltham, and as we pulled into the car park, one of the directors phoned us to say the show had been cancelled. She didn't even have the courtesy to come and speak to us in person! Instead, she simply told us to turn round and go back home. By then we had become very disillusioned by it all. This was not our idea of helping people, and we decided, at this point, to call it a day and go back to our own sittings and meetings.

In May 2005, Lynn (the lady who had received a message from her dad at Retford Town Hall) made contact with us again – this time to see if we would do some private sittings at her home. There were five people to be seen, and there was a lovely atmosphere in the house. The sittings went well.

The fourth person to come into the room was a little lady called Edna. She seemed rather nervous as she sat down. Just as I started to speak, Lynn's two dogs, which were roaming in the garden, started to howl pitifully. As I continued, the howling just got louder. Edna looked at me and grabbed my hand.

'Oh my God, Trace! Isn't that a bad omen?' she asked.

'No, no Edna, don't worry about it,' I said, rather firmly.

'But I *am* worried,' Edna persisted. 'You see, my husband is seriously ill and I wanted to know if he's going to be all right.'

We continued the sitting and reassured Edna that her mum and dad in the spirit world were watching over her, and that her husband was going to be fine. When she left the room, the howling stopped. We later found out that everything turned out well and her husband's health improved, just as we had predicted.

The last lady to be seen was Lynn. Her father came through to talk again, and was able to tell her some amazing things about his own life, and also give her some good advice about what was happening in her life at the time. One of the things that Paul told her concerned a change of job. He told her that she had become disgruntled with her job in a bank and would be starting a new position which was quite different to anything she had done before. He also gave her the date of 13 June. After the sitting Lynn confirmed that on 13 June she was starting a new job as a trainee registrar of births, marriages and deaths. We told her that we had set a date for our wedding, and joked that it would be wonderful if she would be the one to marry us. She said she'd love to, but that she doubted she would be trained in time.

Getting married – and getting back on track

13 August 2005, our wedding day, wasn't a sunny day at all. In fact, it rained so heavily that we thought it would never stop! But imagine our absolute delight when Lynn turned up at the hotel an hour before the wedding and said she would be assisting with our marriage ceremony. Apparently, someone had phoned in sick at the last minute and so she had been asked to step in at short notice. She has since told us that

ours was the first-ever wedding at which she officiated. We thought this was absolutely amazing and surely could not be put down to coincidence.

Our true friends and family, those who had stood by us during the difficult years, were all present to enjoy the celebrations and we both marvelled at the wealth of positive support we had on our special day. Paul's speech after the ceremony brought tears to the eyes of many within the room, mine included.

He told everyone that he had wanted to achieve two things before he reached the age of 40 – one was to stop smoking, the other was to marry a beautiful woman, and he couldn't believe that he had managed to do both! Then he went on to say that even though it was raining outside, the sun had certainly shone for him, as he was sure it had for everyone else when I walked down the aisle to stand by his side.

For our honeymoon, we decided to spend a week with our two dogs Bo and Penny at 'Honeymoon Cottage' in the Yorkshire Dales. It was a beautiful sunny week in fabulous countryside and we idled our days away, walking, relaxing and enjoying the tranquillity.

On our return, we decided it was time to get back on track with our spiritual work and so we handed in our notice at our part-time jobs and set about letting people know we were available again to take bookings.

We also busied ourselves making contact with theatres to book dates for a tour, and designed new posters and leaflets to help promote our work. Whilst working part-time we hadn't been able to do any theatre evenings for a while and it was a huge leap of faith for us to give up our jobs and to try to earn a living from stage shows instead. Although we were slightly apprehensive, something deep inside us told us that this was what we had to do. So we sent out lots of prayers to the spirit world and waited to see what would happen.

We weren't disappointed. It was really good to be out on the road again, doing what we enjoyed most meeting new people and seeing the beautiful English countryside as we passed from town to town.

Just as it did before, the momentum soon picked up. Everywhere we went, our work was really well received.

In October 2005 we were contacted by a company who were planning a TV show for Channel 5, which would challenge psychics to prove that their gifts were real. In the beginning, we were quite interested in taking part; that was until the organisers became very difficult about the timings. We were in the midst of re-establishing ourselves and we were expected to cancel our own events in favour of the TV show, for which we were to receive no payment whatsoever. We just couldn't afford to do this, but the TV company were not in the least bit interested in us as people, only in getting their show out on time.

In the end, we had to pull out, due to other commitments. When we saw the finished product on TV, we were glad we hadn't appeared, as we felt it gave a very poor view of what we do, and didn't really cover all aspects of the work of a psychic or medium.

People first

From time to time, when TV companies contact us with details of programmes they are hoping to make, we consider each one on its merits, whilst seeing if we can fit it in with our own commitments to theatres and individuals who have dates booked in. Obviously, TV is a good way of promoting our work, and showing what we can do to a broader audience, but we believe that people matter most. We thoroughly enjoy working with people in an audience situation or in a one-to-one setting, and it is this kind of work that gives us the most job satisfaction.

This time around, the press have started to take more of an interest in us and our work. They seem particularly keen to focus on the fact that we are both mediums and married. In September 2006 we received a telephone call from a reporter at *Woman's Own* magazine. She had seen our website and wanted to write an article about how we met and fell in love. This article was followed up by similar articles in *The Psychic News, Pick Me Up* magazine and then *Chat It's Fate*.

The media seems fascinated by the fact that we met and fell in love following Nigel's tragic suicide. They often comment that it is as if he guided us to each other. I also like to think this is the case.

Nowadays we are very busy indeed. We are working hard, taking our show around the smaller theatres in the UK – word is getting round and tickets usually sell out fast. The rest of our time we use to help people who need help in coming to terms with losing a loved one. We do not charge these people. We also get involved in charity events, and are sometimes called upon to help people who believe their homes to be haunted. There is so much to do that we often feel there aren't enough hours in the day.

We receive thousands of emails every year from people asking us for help, and many of these come from abroad. At the moment the only way we can help people in other countries is by telephone, but we hope that one day, in the near future, the spirit world will see fit to help us spread our wings a little so that we are able to visit these places in person, and meet some of those other people in far-off countries who need our help.

We spoke to Josie in Tasmania again by telephone in 2007, and once again Eleanor came through with her vibrant personality, giving wonderfully accurate details about the things that had been happening since she had passed away. She also gave new evidence about herself which left Josie in no doubt that Eleanor had been communicating.

Afterwards Josie wrote to us, telling of her experiences with Eleanor and with us as mediums:

My beautiful daughter, Eleanor, was born in March 1995 and I fell in love with her the minute I saw her. I was 35 years old and felt very lucky and blessed.

She was the most beautiful baby, toddler and little girl, and was developing into a gorgeous young lady when she was diagnosed with a malignant brain tumour just before her 10th birthday. We thought this was an out-of-the-blue diagnosis but know now that part of the tumour started at age five when Eleanor had a problem with unresolved vomiting for some time. After many tests and investigations this was decided to be a gastric-type problem and did 'resolve' after some time. The opinion of expert doctors in the paediatric brain tumour area is now that this problem was caused by the brain tumour. The tumour must have been 'dormant' for a few years and then turned very nasty and grew rapidly, which is when we had our terrible diagnosis.

Despite every effort and with the help of expert doctors in Australia and overseas, Eleanor died just less than five months from her diagnosis. She remains our inspiration in everything we do and we miss her more than I could ever put into words. For her younger sister and brother, her father and myself, life will of course never be the same. I used to think my life would never be the same because Eleanor died, but I now know that it will never be the same because she LIVED. We were lucky to be her family, I was lucky to be her mother, and I would not be without the experience of having her in my life for a wonderful 10 years. I could write on and on about her achievements at school, in dancing, in gymnastics and in life in general – she was a beautiful girl inside and out and many notes from her school friends tell of how Eleanor was friendly and funny and kind.

We never told Eleanor of the terrible prognosis we were given – we wanted her to feel positive, plus we hoped always for a miracle. Indeed we thought we found our miracle when the doctors cautiously thought that it may be a slower-growing tumour than that originally diagnosed and therefore may have a better outcome. Devastatingly for all of us, that was not to be.

One day when Eleanor was feeling down and wondering why she had to have this brain tumour I said that if I could have it for her I would (and I'm sure any parent would do the same for their child if they could). She looked at me and said, 'I wouldn't let you.' She was not yet 10 years old at this time but showed maturity many others will not achieve if they live to be 100.

Most grief counsellors will listen to you, let you cry, rant and rave about 'why us?' – but then help you to 'move on' by using various techniques to help you stop dwelling on things and to move on with your life. I know that these sorts of things are not for me. What I need is to know that my wonderful daughter has not really died but has just gone somewhere else where she is happy and that we can be together again one day when my time comes to join her in this other 'place'.

Religion can help (I was brought up Catholic), but relies on 'believing', 'having faith' and 'not questioning'. That's very difficult when you want proof.

And that's where Tracy and Paul came to my rescue. These wonderful, gifted, warm and very caring people are able to give that proof. Some aspects of that information are very clear and some less clear but becoming more so. My girlfriend tried to find a medium she met some years ago – the great Albert Best – only to find out that Albert had himself moved on to that other world. But in searching for him she found Paul and Tracy. So Albert in fact found them for us. And I think Eleanor may have helped out too!

There was a lot of information given which left absolutely no doubt that Eleanor is still with us in spirit – information about her illness, things here at home and school, information about family and friends, not to mention my father being present with her too (my Dad died when Eleanor was 2 and a half but they were very close). After our first contact Paul & Tracy e-mailed me with the exact date of a birthday party we were having (this was for our other daughter and was some time after her actual birthday date). Even my husband, whilst a little sceptical about the work of mediums, could not believe this accuracy and is now a convert!

Both times I have spoken to Tracy and Paul – and remember we are on opposite sides of the world and have never met in person – I have come away convinced that Eleanor is there, using them to communicate with me. I thank Eleanor for finding a way to let me know she is OK and I thank Paul & Tracy for sharing their gift as mediums with myself and with others who so badly need this knowledge – and I thank them for the true compassion with which they do their job. We cried together, we laughed together and I felt they truly understood my need and Eleanor's need and I wish more people could experience the work of Paul & Tracy and other mediums that can bring comfort in knowing that those we love still exist.

With love from Josie

What lies ahead

For us, the future appears bright. We are thankful for the gifts we have, and also the love we are able to share. We hope in our hearts that we will always have the time and energy to be able to support others in their times of trouble, and to point them in the right direction with the help of our friends in the spirit world.

We firmly believe that the spirit world engineered our lives, and brought us together; that working as mediums and being a couple was truly our destiny. Whatever you may think, whatever your reasons for reading our story, we hope we have given a true account of what it is really like to be a medium – an intermediary between this world and the spirit world.

If you are thinking of embarking upon this type of journey yourself, we hope our story will help you to understand some of the pitfalls you may face along the way.

If you are bereaved, and want to know more about whether communication with a loved one is possible, then we hope our story will give you some hope, and encourage you to seek out a medium who might be able to help you.

If you are a sceptic, then maybe we have given you food for thought, a glimmer of interest in a subject you may once have looked upon with derision.

Whichever category you fall into, we wish you well, and maybe one day we will have the chance to meet, and show you how our work has changed our lives, and the lives of others.

We don't consider this to be the end. In fact, it is only the beginning, and one thing is for certain: we will continue to share our experiences with you all, as we start the next chapter on our spiritual journey.

Epilogue

And just to bring you right up to date with what's been happening, and to show you exactly how much our lives are influenced by 'coincidences' and fate, we wanted to tell you a few of the unusual things that happened to us during the process of writing and publishing this book.

After we had finished our draft version of the book in December 2006, we realised that we hadn't really thought about what would happen next. We very much knew that we wanted to share this story with you, but had no idea of how to go about it. We had a look at a few publishers' websites and realised we would probably need a literary agent – so we set to work deciding who best to approach. We soon discovered there were many to choose from, and we didn't have a clue where to start, so one Saturday afternoon we emailed three agents randomly to see what would happen.

One of the people we emailed was Jeffrey Simmons, and he was very keen to see the manuscript. We sent it to him and kept our fingers crossed! About a week later, he telephoned to say that he liked the book, and would like to work with us. We were really pleased, but imagine our absolute amazement when Jeffrey told us he had been the literary agent of Doris Collins and had co-written her books. We were astonished to hear this news, as we hadn't had a clue who Jeffrey was when we first emailed him. But once again we were brought into contact with someone who could not only help us, but who appeared to be another person with a tangible link to our story, and who would fit snugly into the intricate jigsaw of our lives.

Doris Collins had figured largely in Paul's life, and we knew the book would be published after hearing that Jeffrey had been her agent. We just knew in our hearts that it was part of what was meant to be.

Once Piatkus had accepted the book, we had to make some revisions. This turned out to be an interesting process because, one by one, the people we had written about, but not heard from for many years, made contact in a variety of different ways.

Firstly, we were working on the chapter about Paul visiting College Road Spiritualist church, and his friendship with Edie Spooner. In between working on the book, we also had some theatre dates booked. One of these was at Crawley. After the second night, we were packing our belongings and getting ready to leave the theatre when the house manager approached us, stating that someone wished to speak to us – it was Edie Spooner's grand-daughter! We went through to chat to her and her friends, and Edie had sent her love to us both from Doncaster, where she still lives in the same house she lived in when Paul first met her all those years ago. She is also still a regular at College Road Spiritualist church.

About a week later, we were dealing with the next chapter of the book about Paul's time in the development circle, when he used to get a lift with a lady called Pauline. Imagine our absolute astonishment when we opened our emails one morning to find an email from none other than Pauline! She has moved out of Doncaster now and is doing really well. She told us that she was also writing a book.

Whilst we were making some changes to the chapter about Paul's first public meeting at the Fairway Hotel, Pam, the lady he'd met there and become friends with, also made contact. This time it was a telephone call quite out of the blue. She had moved house some time ago, and we'd lost contact with her, but then – lo and behold – she phoned us, and at exactly the same time that we were dealing with the information about her in the book. She has stopped doing her Tarot card readings now, and helps her new husband with his property developing business, which keeps her extremely busy.

This is getting really strange, we thought. Could anyone else possibly make contact? Oh yes, they could! About a week later, Tracy literally bumped into her old friend Chris Merrick in the centre of Worksop – you guessed it, right at the point when we were revising the chapter about Tracy joining the healing circle that Chris ran with Matt. The last time we saw Chris was at our wedding in 2005. Sadly, we lost touch with her after that. We were upset to learn that Chris has been unwell since, but is now on the road to recovery, and we were really thrilled to be back in touch with her again.

As we edited the section in our book about Lynn, who we'd met after an evening at Retford Town Hall, and who also officiated at our marriage, we quite literally bumped into her in the supermarket that very same day. Again, we hadn't seen or heard from her since our wedding day in August 2005.

Finally, and perhaps most intriguingly, Tracy's son Luke received a phone call inviting him to go and play with some friends from his primary school one Saturday afternoon in July, just after we had finished all the revisions to the book. When we went to pick him up, he came rushing over to the car with his friends and announced, 'Mum, guess what?' We looked over at the lads expectantly. 'Darren's my cousin!'

Darren is the son of one of Nigel's former girlfriends. Apparently, she has just told Darren that Nigel is his father, and Darren really wanted to get in touch with Luke to let him know.

All of this meant such a lot to us and we like to think that the spirits, who have watched over us and brought us to where we are now, were giving us their final stamp of approval, and reminding us how lucky we have been to have received so much wonderful help from so many people along the way.

We will certainly do our best to cherish those new people who have come into our lives during the publishing process, and will remain in contact with those who have come back into our lives whilst the work was in progress.